What People Are Saying About This Book

"Chris Gregas has done a great job pointing the reader toward the truth of our identity in Christ. In a day where so many sincere believers are trying to establish their identity by their religious performance, here is a book that reminds us that our value is based on what He has done and not what we do. If you want to be encouraged by the grace of God or if you know somebody who needs to be set free from the chains of legalism and begin to walk in the freedom grace brings, The Identity Driven Life *is a key that will release them to know what He wants us all to know and to be all that He wants us to be. I highly recommend it."*

Steve Mcvey,
President of Grace Walk Ministries

"What we do doesn't determine who we are. Who we are determines what we do, so knowing who we are in Christ will greatly impact how we live. Chris Gregas has written a fine book about our identity in Christ and that is critical, because no person can consistently live in a way that is inconsistent with what they believe about themselves."

Dr. Neil T. Anderson,
Founder and President Emeritus of
Freedom in Christ Ministries

"For most people in the church, living out of their new identities in Christ is a very real struggle. Without thinking about it or challenging it, identities are typically shaped by past sins, hurts, or failures. Then we move forward to define ourselves by our giftedness, ability to perform, what we possess, or what people say about us. All of these are dangerous traps, as guilt and condemnation inevitably follow, due to their conditional

nature. *Chris Gregas introduces a good Biblical approach to discovering our new identity in Jesus Christ, based on what He has already accomplished on our behalf, and then living out of that newness. Identity precedes actions. Chris offers the reader a concise look at the meaning and implications of being in Christ and the transformation that can follow."*

Darren Shelburne,
Area Director at
Young Life Gloucester County, New Jersey

"Chris Gregas has hit the nail on the head on one of the most crucial aspects of our spiritual development! Understanding our identity in Christ is the difference maker between doing things for Jesus versus doing things with him. If you've discovered God's purposes for your life, but were left feeling inadequate to achieve them, read this book and learn the core truths that can change your life!"

Pastor Brian Moss,
Lead pastor of Oak Ridge Baptist Church
in Salisbury, Maryland.

"My husband (Chris) has been a faithful teacher for as long as I have known him on spiritual identity. I have seen a transformation in my own life over the years as I've understood what God thinks of me and seeing him live out the words of this book. Every Christian will be changed in their mind and heart through reading this. What God thinks of us matters most. Thanks Chris for writing this for the body of Christ."

Janet Gregas,
wife of the author

The Identity Driven Life

Why Knowing WHO You Are Is Just As Important As Knowing WHY You Are

Chris J. Gregas

Clovercroft Publishing

THE IDENTITY DRIVEN LIFE: WHY KNOWING WHO YOU ARE IS AS IMPORTANT AS KNOWING WHY YOU ARE

©2015 by Chris J. Gregas

Published by Clovercroft Publishing, Franklin, Tennessee. Published in association with Larry Carpenter of Christian Book Services, LLC. www.christianbookservices.com

Edited by Gail Fallen

Cover Design by Tom Miller

Interior Design by Adept Concept Solutions

Printed in the United States of America

978-1-940262-98-7

This book is **dedicated** to my best friend and bride of twenty five years—Janet Gregas. She has been with me every step of the way and has faithfully encouraged me to finish the book and share it with the masses. Her own brave acceptance of the identity truths in her own life has made me a glad proponent of its life giving truths these many years to so many. I love you more!

It is also **dedicated** to my four beloved children who have always acted like they are listening to my regular talks and sermons on the subject of identity and who are, I'm sure, glad that this book is finally available to the masses. Thanks Alicia, Andrew, Aaron & Ashlyn. I love with all my heart.

Acknowledgments

This book was written on the shoulders of many people that have proven to be a great blessing in my life.

First, I am thankful for my late mom and dad for always believing in me even when I didn't believe in myself and for encouraging me to write and write some more.

Next, I am grateful to my college roommate, Paul Fitzpatrick, who help start my on the road to spiritual transformation through knowing our identity in Christ.

I am thankful to Larry Carpenter, President of Clovercroft Publishing and his fine staff for believing in this project and for helping me get it to the finish line.

I am thankful to the many people who encouraged me all along the way to write this book. You know who you are.

I am thankful to my loving congregation at SonRise Christian Fellowship for encouraging me and listening to me as I forged this book out before them.

I am thankful to Miles Stanford and Dr. Neil Anderson for faithfully getting the truths of our identity in Christ out to the masses.

Lastly and mostly, I am thankful to the Lord Jesus Christ for all that He accomplished on the cross for us so that we could have our true identity in Him and in Him—alone.

Contents

Introduction   ix

1   What Is the Identity Driven Life?   1

Part I
Laying the Foundation and Order of
    Spiritual Identity   27

2   Laying the Only Proper Spiritual Foundation
    We Can Lay   29

3   God's Order in the Newer Testament (Part 1)   45

4   God's Order in the Newer Testament (Part 2)   57

5   What Really Happened at Your Salvation?   69

Part II
Five Principles about Spiritual Identity That
    Every Christian Must Know and Understand   85

Identity Truth #1
You Are Who God Says You Are   86

6   Suffering from Spiritual Identity Theft   87

7   Who in God's Name Are You   101

8   The Key to Freedom: Trading Lies for the Truth   119

Identity Truth #2
You Are Unconditionally Loved by the
    One Who Counts   151

9   The Unconditional Love of God   153

10   Abba Father Love—Yes!   167

11   Preparing for Book Two   185

Scripture Index & Scriptural Inferences   193

About the Author   195

Introduction

Maybe you are familiar with the old adage, "You can't teach and old dog new tricks." That may be true in the dog kingdom, but I know it is not wholly true in the human kingdom. We have all learned "new tricks" along life's journey because we saw the need to do so. We sensed the payoff in it, so we allowed something or someone to take us places that we would have never gone ourselves.

Thousands of years of civilization have come and gone, and we humans still make a living out of repeating the same mistakes over and over. The old way is what we like. The new is what we tend to shun. Old shoes or a good old pair of pants are comfortable and familiar. When we are forced to start over or buy new or change even slightly, we naturally find ourselves rebelling against the process. The flesh is ever seeking the easy path and is content on "grinding it out," however miserable it may be, until Jesus comes.

This book and the one after it, which is part two of the same message, will summarize what I just said. Most of us have been used to living a certain way as a Christian man or woman. If you have been in any religious system for more than a few years, you have arrived at a comfort zone of what you know and what you will accept as "added" truth—beyond what you know. Your funnel for receiving "new tricks" is really narrow. Not impossible, but not probable either. It is a funnel that is very hard and crusty and inflexible, and that is often the barrier to us learning and receiving the "whole truth and nothing but the truth" of God. The Holy Spirit's desire—and mine—is for you to become all that God meant for you. If God did not have a purpose for you beyond your own salvation, then you would have been instantly transported to heaven in a flash. But that didn't happen, so we must ask the question, "Is there more for me and you to know and do until we meet Christ?" Well, I think you know the answer to that, and we are going to answer these questions and many more in this book and its sequel.

Our Lord's half-brother James reminds us that every temptation that seeks our destruction is not from GOD, but from our enemy SATAN. I can tell you now, Satan is not happy that you are reading this book. I know that because he is a liar and the Father of Lies. (John 8:44) He does not want you to walk in the truth found in the pages of Scripture or in these pages. He will try to dismiss anything and everything about this book. But I challenge you to work through his smoke and mirrors. Do not listen to the "voices" of defeat and discouragement. Some of you, maybe many of you, are right on the doorstep of spiritual freedom in your life, and this book (and the one that follows) just may be the tool that God uses to spring the freedom door open for you to walk through.

Would you pray this prayer with me as we begin this journey? It is a prayer you can come back to if you wish. It is a prayer that will center your mind and heart on what God wants to do in your life and also on what Satan wants to do if you let him.

Heavenly Father. Thanks for allowing me to be your beloved child and a worker in your kingdom. I want to read this book with the Holy Spirit's insight. I want to be changed from the inside out. I want to know your truth, and I want to stop living by the lies that I have come to believe. Father, I pray that as I read this book, the scales of deception might fall from my eyes and that Jesus Christ, who is my life (Col. 3:4), might become the main source and strength of my Christian walk. I refuse to believe and listen to the lies of Satan, and I know that he desires to destroy my testimony for Christ. Thank you for hearing my prayer and for working in me the life that wins. I give you all the praise for all that you will do. In the name of Jesus. Amen.

1

What Is the Identity Driven Life Anyway?

"It's in Christ that we find out who we are [**identity**] and what we are living for [**purpose**]..."

—Ephesians 1:11
(The Message; emphasis mine)

"Losing identity with nothing to replace it can cause massive damage to the self-concept, and few can tolerate it. However, God does not ask us just to lose our identity but to exchange it for one that will work both for time and eternity."

—Charles Solomon

Like many of you who are reading this book, I too have been beat up by Mr. Life more often than I am comfortable with. Anyone who said that life is free from deep problems surely must have lived and died all on the same day! If you ever have had to face any physical "close calls," you will identify with my story.

Back in early 2010 is when my somewhat comfortable life really started to heat up. I have had my share of stomach issues for as long as I can remember. In my 30s, I was diagnosed as lactose intolerant, and knowing that allowed me to adjust my life accordingly. Yet in early 2010, I woke up from a rare nap one day with a rapid heartbeat of about 140 beats per minute. If you have ever experienced a rapid heartbeat, you know the panic that sets in is nerve-wracking. After an extended period of this, I made my way to the local hospital. After a few days of tests, they diagnosed me with a severe gas lock and sent me packing with a prescription to fill.

I wish my story ended there. It doesn't. Fast-forward a few months later. I was now an interim pastor in a church. Each Sunday when I got up to preach, my heart rate would spike into the high 140s and stay there. At first I reasoned that my arch-enemy Satan was trying to work me over because God was using me. Though that was definitely part of it, something else was seriously wrong as well! Panic attacks were soon the norm, and I had never, up to that point, *ever* experienced a panic attack in my life. Deep worry and fear were just as pronounced in my daily routine, and that had never been a problem in my life either. I was facing something altogether new, and my spiritual identity and value was under siege big time. I daily sought the Lord on what He might be orchestrating, but His silence seemed to reign, so I was in waiting mode once again. It was by far the greatest challenge of my life, but as you now know, I am standing today strong in the Lord . . . only by the mercy and grace of God.

What I am going to talk to you about in this book *works*! It works because the Scriptures scream its workability and because experience sounds its battle cry. I have learned over the four-plus decades of my life that when the towel is available to throw in the ring, it is always too *soon* to do so. But I have also learned that when I look to myself or to those around me to "fix" me or my dreadful situation, then I am headed for multiplied trouble, and so are you!

We are going to discover in this book and the one that follows how we can never (you heard me right— *never*!) define our true self-image or value by or within "ourselves." I know this seems to be a contradiction to all that you have heard, but for the child of God, we are compelled to measure "us" on a whole other level. The sad truth is the great enemy of our souls, Satan, has done a pretty masterful job for centuries stealing people's spiritual identities. I remind you that Christ did not come to Earth merely to prepare us to rediscover our true identity. He came to let us *redefine* them within the confines of His victorious work on a bloodstained tree.

That is what we will celebrate. But like any worthwhile party or celebration, we must witness the good, the bad, and . . . *the ugly!* The exciting thing is that if we are willing to "keep it real," then the end product will be more beautiful than we could have ever imagined.

The power and discouragement of having our identity stolen cannot be underemphasized. Spiritual thievery from the Father of Lies is the oldest form of robbery there is. The sad part is the Devil has not changed his agenda for thousands of years. Why?

Because he doesn't have to. We are often none the wiser to his deception, but I think it is high time the body of Christ uncovers and overcomes his dirty rotten plans!

I read a story about a beast named "Tiger" not long ago that I think really sums up our tenacious struggle to see ourselves truly through God's eyes.

After years of terrorizing the countryside, hunting deer, poaching livestock, and killing game, Tiger grew long in the tooth. Finally, he knew it was time to retire. So he packed his bag: "Poor self-esteem? Check. Poor body image? Check? Poor self-image? Check. Self-portrait? Uh . . . oh well, three out of four ain't bad."

Tiger ambled into town and came to stand before the Three Little Pigs Retirement Home Inc. He rang the bell, and the first little pig appeared on the landing above. "What do you want?" asked the little pig.

"I come here to retire," Tiger replied. "Ooooh. I don't think so," the little pig declared. "You're not like us. You've got big teeth. Very dangerous. We can't let you in."

Tiger, having a poor self-image, went to the dentist to improve these apparent deficiencies and had his teeth removed. The next day, he returned to the Three Little Pigs Retirement Home Inc. "What do you want?" asked the second little pig.

"I have no more teeth. I come here to retire," Tiger replied once more. "Ooooh. No, no, no. That just won't do," the little pig exclaimed. "You're different. You have sharp claws. You scare us. We can't let you in."

Tiger took his poor self-esteem and even worse body-image to the manicurist and had his claws removed. The next day, he returned to the Three Little Pigs Retirement Home Inc. "What do you want?" demanded the third little pig.

"I have no more claws. I come here to retire," Tiger repeated. "Ooooh. Let me see," the little pig muttered as he disappeared from sight. Tiger heard much whispering and commotion behind the big wooden doors. "OK, come in," said the little pig. Tiger strolled through the doors, and there stood the three little pigs, grinning from ear to ear. Suddenly, they jumped on Tiger. Squealing with delight, they beat him up and sent him packing. No teeth. No claws. Yippee! Finally, they got even with Tiger for terrorizing the animals.

Tiger should have known better. He should have accepted who he was and not try to conform to someone else's image of him. What tiger in his right mind lets a pig paint his portrait? He should have painted a self-portrait instead.

Do you seek to improve your body or your body image? Do you seek to improve your claws or your nails, or do you seek to improve your self-esteem? **What do you see when you look in the mirror? So, who paints your portrait?**[1] (emphasis mine).

One of the reasons why I love that story is because it speaks so personally to me. As a young man, I became intimately aware of being confused about who I was. Understanding my true identity has been for me an agonizing journey fighting through the thick haze of self-hate! And, if I could ask *you* personally, I am relatively certain that many of you could relate to the Tiger story and to mine as well. Try as we might, we are often very unsuccessful in defining our "real selves."

[1] David Leonhardt, "Who paints your portrait?" In *Climb Your Stairway to Heaven* (Bloomington, IN: iUniverse, 2001), 66–79.

Being comfortable in our "own skin" can prove to be rather tricky. Unfortunately, the world at large, and often even those closest to us, have successfully wrapped us around their fingers. In the end, we end up becoming the sum total of all that they think and say about us. The result is predictable: *Our real identity is hijacked,* slowly but surely!

An Initial Word about Identity Theft

You probably are aware that identity theft has been a major problem the world over. It has ruined lives, marriages, and businesses in ways that we could never begin to measure. Just the stroke of a keypad or a stolen wallet can cause a person or family to spend the next few years facing pending financial collapse. If you have ever been down that road, you know firsthand what I am talking about.

Yet, I submit that there is even a more subtle and far-reaching "identity theft" going on in the lives of God's children. This theft of identity has infiltrated the body of Christ like a lethal disease, and it is showing in ways that have devastated the church the world over.

As a pastor and spiritual leader for a few decades now, I believe this spiritual waywardness has to first lie squarely at the feet of every true spiritual leader. We are responsible before God to declare and relay the truth of God's word clearly to those who are under our care. That includes teaching the flock the power and place of "Christ identity" in their walk. Instead, we have far too often skated over the *order* that God has laid out in His word and replaced it with an order that is highly cultural or pragmatic at best.

What is that "order," you may ask?

The order of *being* and then *doing* as a child of God. The order of seeing ourselves the way God sees us first so we can model to the culture clearly who exactly our source of identity and strength is. I do not believe the blame falls totally on spiritual leaders though. It falls on every one of us who seek to make a name for ourselves rather than being passionate about exalting the Name that is above every name (Phil. 2:9–10).

Proverbs 29:18 declares that "Where there is no prophetic vision the people cast off restraint" (ESV). That verse is alive and well today. The present culture of Christianity, especially in the West, is in dire need of change and transformation. Inner *deformity* must be exchanged for inner *transformity*, and time is of the essence.

The identity driven life is a clear call to all those who identify *with* Christ to find their identity *in* Christ. I like to say it this way: Knowing who you are (identity) is just as important as knowing why you are (purpose). Both are important to living a successful Christian life, but one has to come before the other. In God's playbook, identity must always lead purpose and not the other way around. But spiritual identity unfortunately has a proven track record of trailing way behind purpose. Yet, our knowledge and application of what God says about us as His people is just as valuable (maybe more so) than what we could ever do for God in this life. I am afraid that many Christians may be hot on their purpose but cold as to why they are doing or not doing what they should.

In these writings, you will discover life-giving truths from the New Testament that have the potential of leading you to the place where you can trade in your faulty, unreliable self-esteem for something eternally better and certainly more enduring. The divine knowledge and subsequent feeling that you are special, loved, worthy, and significant must come from the right source and spring or we will, like our dark culture, grasp at things, experiences, and achievements to try to fill the great eternal void within. In this book, we will focus primarily on Identity Truths 1 and 2. We will look at Identity Truths 3, 4, and 5 in the next book. These truths will be the bread and butter of what we are going to discover.

My prayer is that by reading these books, you will begin or deepen your appreciation of what God really thinks about you and what that looks like in your everyday walk with Him. May God grant that for every last one of us!

The Purpose Driven Life Explained

Many of us have probably read, or at least heard of, the award-winning Christian book *The Purpose Driven Life*, written by Pastor Rick Warren. This book, which was originally published in 2002 and re-released in 2012, was introduced to the religious audience like a crashing meteor. Unarguably, it made an indelible mark upon the Christian church and even secular academia literally the world over. Warren's devotional style of writing and his fondness for engaging the reader made this book desirable in almost every sector of society. What you may not be aware of is that the "felt need," or hot button, in the late 1990s was a word that Warren picked up on and wrote about: *purpose!*

People all over the world need purpose for their lives. Without it we are aimlessly wandering through life with little direction. It is no great surprise that Warren's book and premise was widely received and broadly accepted. Warren opens up the book with a profile of what "drives" our lives." He says that all of us are driven by "something" or even a list of "somethings" in life that give it purpose and meaning. Think about it. *Isn't your life "driven" by something?*

It may be a quest for self-pleasure and happiness. Or maybe by what others say about you or think of you. Some of us are driven through life by the passion to be the best, running over all those who may be in our way. What is it in your life? It's something or someone, I promise you that.

Since God is a God of order, all that He does has deep meaning and purpose. Our feelings and experiences may tell us different, but the Bible is wildly firm on this. As we begin this book, we need to see how this order plays into what I have come to call the "identity driven life." So I ask you: Is knowing *"why* we are" what God **first** intends for us to know as His children? Does purpose lead identity, or does identity propel purpose? Does what we believe about ourselves have anything to do with how and what we become? That is what we want to answer and affirm.

The Identity Driven Life Explained

Let me define what I mean by "identity" at the start. Our perceived identity is how we see or view ourselves.

It is what we use to define our worth or value in this world. It is what we feel about ourselves based our own conclusions and often based on what others have said about us. I think you would agree that our perceived identity may be the most important concept we come to terms with for our lives.

Recently, I came across a product that is all natural and unbelievable in its ability to relieve physical pain. I don't have much physical pain, but my wife is another story. She has (due to a lot of childhood injuries, etc.) lived with pain most of her adult life, and for the last seven or so years, it has been *chronic*. So, a business partner of mine calls me one day and tells me about how this pain patch has worked for him. Right away I think—I wonder if it could help MY WIFE! We needed a breakthrough, to be sure.

So I ordered it because the pain medications had run their course and the doctor said that she could not take them anymore because they were making her sick. We got the package a few days later, and she put this all-natural "power patch" on. To our amazement, she was totally relieved of her back and sciatic pain. She has now (as of this writing) been pain-free for almost four months, and she has her physical life back. Amazing. I have since learned that the company has a motto that is in response to people asking, "Where do I put this patch?" Their response is a simple one: "Stick it where it hurts."

I have asked myself and the Lord, "Do we as believers in Christ have anything that we can give to calm or relieve the emotional and spiritual hurt and pain of people? Do we have something that people can receive that will allow them to "stick it where it hurts"?

I believe we do! The spiritual, all-supernatural patch we have is called **the identity driven life** message. This teaching and way of life will get to the deepest pain and hurt of mankind and bring the healing power of Christ to their weary, worn souls. Praise His amazing Name!

So what do I mean by **the "identity driven life"**? What is it and what is it *not*? How does it manifest itself in our Christian walk?

What It Is

It is a life lived by the Christian that is rooted in the person and work of Jesus Christ on the cross and through the empty tomb. Our spiritual identity and its possibility are solely due to the bloodshed of Christ on the cross, and because three days later, he rose from the grave proving He was God (Rom. 1:4). Jesus lived an exemplary life, and His miracles and divine works were unmatched— *yes*! Yet His life is not what defines our importance or value. Walking in the steps of Jesus or imitating Him is admirable, but any soul can do that and yet never find the true meaning of their "true value." It is the cross and the tomb and the believer's connection to it which seals the deal of the Father's love and opinion of us.

What It Is Not

It is *not* a life lived by the Christian that egotistically makes them feel better or believing that they are better than everyone else. Our spiritual identity has nothing to do with us or our varied talents or abilities. We are not valuable because we are good. We are good because, in Christ, we are valuable. Valuable enough to be repeatedly called so throughout the whole New Testament. Do not be deceived into thinking that this book is all about making ourselves a better version of ourselves. *It is the exact opposite.* Our celebrated place in the Father's house is not to rub it in the face of those who are *outside* the door. In the end, we are just redeemed beggars telling other unredeemed beggars were to find the "Living Bread."

What It Is

It *is* a life lived by the Christian with the truth of what God thinks of us in Christ as the motivating factor of our lives. As we will discuss later in detail, we are either going to believe what God says about us or what others believe about us. Once we begin to trust heavily in the God's final verdict about us, then we can never be the same, and it will produce a joy and a peace that we have possibly never known. These truths of Scripture are just not another "piece" of character or spiritual truth to file in our spiritual notebooks. It is the very motivation to do what God has destined for us to do. It is what we were called to be.

What It Is Not

It is *not* a life lived by Christians who fail to realize they are entirely spiritually bankrupt and totally spiritually lost apart from the grace and work of Christ. The identity driven life is a life lived with full knowledge of "but for the grace of God, there go I." It is a life that is lived free from the idea that our self-sufficiency and material riches can add one thing to what Christ accomplished on the cross for us.

What It Is

It is the Christian coming to the realization that their value, worth, love, and acceptance can only be found in who they are in Christ now that they have been born-again. Our spiritual identity is found only in Christ and not even in our real value as a human being. That is where "self-esteem" speech gets it all wrong. For the Christian, it is not self-esteem but rather "Christ-esteem" that registers in the corridors of heaven. We will learn later that our "self" has nothing to offer us when we register and start attending classes in Christ's school of discipleship.

What It Is Not

It is *not* a life lived by the Christian with a disregard for service for the Lord or for a casual view of what we do for God and its effects. The identity driven life is not a life of spiritual ease and inactivity. It is possibly a life with *more* activity for the Lord, but this activity is centered in the power of the Holy Spirit. It is not because we seek to be accepted by God by what we do, but that we fully realize that we are accepted by God because of what Christ did! The identity driven life is what God intended for us to live out so that we could accomplish the good things that He has laid out for us in Christ (Eph. 2:10).

Sinners or Saints? Which Is It?

In understanding our true identity, we must talk about our relationship to sin and what God does for us when we are saved by His grace. So what exactly does God say about our relationship to sin now that we are His? I begin with a question:

How many times does God call us who are His children "sinners" in the New Testament?

I have lived mostly in two different church cultures in my lifetime. The first was a culture where just about everything you did was sinful and we were dirty, scum-of-the-earth sinners and God was eternally not happy at all with us. Being "sin consciousness" was definitely the overriding smell that permeated my life as a new believer in Christ in this culture.

But I have also come to experience "another" religious culture where sin was not that big a deal, and in fact, God merely winks at it because His love overlooks it. Today more than ever, we seem to have a generation of believers that eat, drink, and sleep religious experience and cheap grace. Listen: I am a grace guy through and through. You will be convinced of that when you finish this book and the next, but we need to remember that in every generation, sin has not changed, either to God or according to His standards. Sin is real—yes, yes, and *yes*—but there is a remedy for sin, and that is the great news. So both paradigms "swings" (legalism or license) are equally destructive to our growth as a child of God. So I ask the question again:

How many times does God call His children "sinners" in the New Testament?

Zero is the answer. Yes. You read that right. Now some of you sharp shooters might say, "Doesn't the epistle of James mentions believers being 'sinners' twice?" (4:8 and 5:20).

Well, the question is: Who is James talking to? Saints who sin or sinners that are not yet saints? I believe Dr. Neil Anderson and Dr. Robert Saucy, in their book *The Common Made Holy*, make this distinction crystal clear when they write:

> The only other places in Scripture that may refer to Christians as sinners are both in the book of James. The first, "Wash your hands, you sinners" (James 4:8), is one of ten verbal commands urging anyone who reads this general epistle to make a decisive break with the old life. We believe this is best understood as calling the reader to repentance and therefore salvation. The second use of "sinner" (James 5:20) appears to be a reference to unbelievers as well. The "sinner" is to be turned from the error of his ways and thus be saved from "death." Since this verse is most likely referring to spiritual death, it suggests that the person was not a believer. In both instances, James was using the term "sinner" as it was used, particularly among the Jews, to speak of those "who disregarded the law of God and flouted standards of morality." The fact that these sinners are among those addressed by James does not necessarily mean that they are believers, for Scripture teaches that unbelievers can be among the saints (see 1 John 2:19), as they surely are today in our churches. Referring to them as sinners fits the usual description of those who have not

come to repentance and faith in God, since the rest of Scripture clearly identifies believers as saints who still have the capacity to sin.[2]

Someone might say, "Paul called himself the *'chiefest of sinners'* didn't he?" He did, but it seems clear that Paul was talking about what he was and is without the grace of God working in his life. Remember, pre-salvation, Paul was a self-righteous bigot who thought he was doing God a favor by extinguishing out all those of "the Way." Paul overwhelmingly lays out the argument of seeing ourselves "new in Christ and free from sin" more than any other New Testament writer. He had a tremendous balance with both his real sinfulness apart from Christ and His lofty spiritual position with and in Christ. We must as well.

His reminder of "if anyone is in Christ, he is a new creation" (2 Cor. 5:17, ESV) is a vivid reminder of who we *now* are as opposed to what we once *were*. We may not be what we *ought* to be in Christ, but thank God we are not what we *used* to be before Christ invaded our spirits! For those who want to say that this "identity message" gives undeserved worth to fallen man and downplays his hopeless state in sin, I would ask this simple question: Why can't spiritual worth and spiritual lostness dwell in the same room? Go with me on this.

We can and must readily and fully support the biblical truth of the total spiritual lostness of man outside of Christ. Yet we must also recognize that

---

[2] Neil Anderson and Robert Saucy, *The Common Made Holy*, English Language ed. (Eugene, OR: Harvest House, 1997), 43.

the New Covenant brought the liberating message of the total acceptance and security of every man, woman, and child *if* (don't miss that important preposition) they are indeed "in Christ." In other words, we must teach both because *both* are taught in the New Testament. The absence of spiritual identity teaching isn't that it is teaching that is little known or even a small part of New Testament character, as some have claimed. The problem is, we have largely ignored it for so long that its message is today "hard" to receive.

What Do Identity and Sainthood Have in Common?

Since believers in Christ are not called "sinners" at all in the New Testament, does that mean *God* minimizes sin in the life of the believer? Listen to what Paul says in response to this question: "Well then, should we keep on sinning so that God can show us more and more of his wonderful grace? Of course not!" (Rom. 6:1-2a, NLT). In other words, kill the thought. It is a very strong word in the original Greek language! He continues, "How shall we who died to sin live any longer ruled by it?" (Rom. 6:1-2, Gregas Paraphrase). Yet, isn't it interesting that the Holy Spirit (the "Divine Author" of the Scriptures according to 2 Tim. 3:16-17) does not label us as active, positional "sinners" not once? I bet (like me) you thought it was a whole lot more. That is because in our churches, we seem to be more "sin conscious" than we are "saint conscious." According to the New Testament, that ought not to be the case.

Again, I don't want you to miss the big picture. Do I believe that Christians sin? Of course I do. First John 1:8–10 answers that question. Do I believe that Christians can live "ugly" lives at different times in their lives? I have unfortunately seen it, and besides, it's clearly supported by the Scriptures (i.e. the Corinthian believers, for starters). Do I believe that the Scriptures teach true and real "repentance" is needed for true Christians? Yes I do, and I am willing to bet that most of us reading this book have very little understanding of the term "repentance," let alone its powerful implications. It is a sign of the times in our churches, to be sure.

I go back to the question I asked earlier. How many times does God call us, we who are His children, "sinners" in the New Testament?

Let me go a step further and bring this full circle so we can begin to build a strong case for the identity driven life.

How many times does the New Testament call believers in Christ "saints" or those who are "sanctified"?

Take a guess and don't look below. Not once, not twice, not even ten times, though would you not admit, that ten times would be a lot? Ready for the answer? It may floor you as it did me the first time I discovered it. I count over *sixty* times in the King James Version of the New Testament.

Can you believe that? It's hard to believe, but it is the complete truth. You say, "I can't believe it." Well, I hate to break it to you, but just because you can't or won't believe it doesn't negate its truth one inch. You see, our feelings, our doubts, or even our inability to receive this awesome truth does not weaken its divine reality in the least. Don't ever forget that God's word (His final account) is "settled" (fixed or completed) in heaven (Psalm 119:89). We are never told to approach God's word as something that "submits" to our thinking or lifestyle, but instead, we are to "submit" to its life-giving message. When we do, we become freer than we could ever imagine.

What Does a Saint Look Like in the New Testament?

No doubt some of you grew up with a bent towards religious "saints." That saints are *made,* not *born.* I mean how many saints do you think you saw growing up? The truth is, a lot more than you think! A saint is widely accepted as someone who has lived an extraordinary religious life, was a worker of miracles on some level, and went straight to heaven when he or she died. Right? Well, you'll be relieved to know that the Bible does *not* paint that portrait. In fact, it flatly rejects the idea that real saints are made by the way they live or die. In fact, the Bible says that saints are actually "born," or better said, "reborn," and not *made* at all. Some of you need to take a breath. The Bible sums up sainthood this way: Saints by calling and grace, not by works or performance. We become saints by Christ's work, not by ours.

If you are still having trouble with the statement "saints are not made but born," let me challenge you further so we can wrap this chapter up on the same page.

Question: Who were the most fleshly, misguided, childish, and immature believers in the New Testament? And the answer: The Corinthian church.

They had more problems than a mathematician! In fact, Paul lays them out spiritually in both of his recorded letters to them. This church was severely fractured by divisions, filled with arrogance, seemingly supportive of immorality, involved in legal troubles with other believers, and struggling over whether sexual relations were appropriate within the husband-wife relationship. Additionally, they were abusing the Lord's Supper, taking unhealthy advantage of their Christian freedom, and had a real imbalance over spiritual gifts and the future bodily resurrection of believers. If you were a pastor or someone looking for a new church home, knowing this, would that motivate you to pursue this fellowship's weekly company? I think not.

So be amazed at what Paul says to them in his first letter. It is not the emphasis that you might have guessed.

Paul summoned by the will and purpose of God to be an apostle (special messenger) of Christ Jesus, and our brother, Sosthenes, To the church (assembly) of God which is in Corinth, to those consecrated and purified and made holy in Christ Jesus, [who are] selected and called to be saints (God's people), together with all those who in any place call upon and give honor to the name of our Lord Jesus Christ, both their Lord and ours: Grace (favor and spiritual blessing) be to you and [heart] peace from God our Father and the Lord Jesus Christ. (1 Cor. 1:1–3, AMP)

"Called to be saints": *Really*, Paul? Yes, because remember, true sainthood had to do with who they were, and it has to do with who we are if Jesus knows us. These verses only prove a powerful underlying truth . . . the very basis for this book.

Sainthood had to do with who they *were*, and it has to do with who we *are* if Jesus knows us.

That is, in fact, our truest spiritual identity. Sinners, yes; but that is not what we are by position or standing *now*. We have come out of spiritual darkness into the light of Christ! (Col. 1:13). We are saints of the living God, and because we are, we can be "set apart" to do the good things that God has for us. Don't miss the order! We will learn in this book that who we really are in Christ has nothing to do with what we've done, what we do, or what we fail to do.

Concluding Remarks about the Identity Driven Life

When you boil the identity driven life down to the bare minimum, here's what you get:

First, identity has to do with our "being" while purpose has to do with our "doing." Put another way, identity has to do with the *character* of Christ wrought within us, while purpose focuses in on the *conduct* of the believer wrought from us. I know that seems to be simplistic, but it is nonetheless true.

In his book *Who Do You Think You Are*, pastor and writer Mark Driscoll discusses this when he writes:

> As a pastor, I've spent years seeking to help people meet Jesus and experience the life transformation he alone can accomplish. I consistently see people who wrongly but earnestly seek to change their behavior rather than first understand their identity. But God knows that what you do flows from who you are. As Christians, we live from our identity. We are defined by who we are in Christ, not what we do or fail to do for Christ. Christ defines who we are by who he is and what he's done for us, in us and through us. Understanding this information is the key to your transformation.[3]

Second, identity is *positional* in nature. Positional means that it is a fixed, unalterable chair that God has seated us in. This fixed position rests completely and only on the work of Christ for us. It has nothing to do with our occasional ugliness or lack of service for God. Our conduct is something altogether different from our position. Who we are can never be confused with what we do, but we will learn that they both have a blessing from God—if they work in harmony!

Finally, when we talk of an identity message, we are NOT talking about a message that is laced with a "prosperity" ending. What do I mean by that?

---

[3] Mark Driscoll, *Who Do You Think You Are?* (Nashville: Thomas Nelson, 2013), 19.

There has been a quiet but definitive movement towards spiritual identity lately that is "spiritual" in nature, but not borne of the Holy Spirit. The unholy spirit has warped and twisted the beautiful identity message into a "me first" extravaganza. Prosperity and blessing are the bywords, and money is the end game. I am not going to name names—though I would not feel out of place to do so—but the "prosperity gospel" that has taken root in Christendom, literally the world over, is false, demonic in nature, and an ingenious imposter of the real message. How can we tell if the message of identity is the "real message" and not a false one?

First, the identity message in the New Testament and throughout this book is rooted in the cross work of Jesus Christ. Yes, we are recipients of that work. Yes, our spiritual value flows from that work but it is ONLY because of that sacred work. When we start to tell people that they are the "head and not the tail" so that they can buy a new top of the line BMW or a Malibu beach house or so they can get out of poverty, we have successfully perverted the message, and we have effectively aided the enemy in egregious falsehood.

Second, financial prosperity has NOTHING to do with our spiritual identity. Some of the greatest saints of biblical times and throughout history have been some of the most financially strapped of this world, but they were rich where it matters most—in *faith*. (That is what James says in his letter.) I know that there are plenty of teachers out there today saying that poverty is of the Devil and that God saved us to prosper in "every area" of our lives. That just doesn't wash, scripturally. I wish it did for a host of reasons. The common truth is . . .

God has indeed blessed us in abundance, but according to Ephesians 1:3, it is a blessing that is *spiritual* in nature. Money can certainly be a blessing, and there is certainly nothing wrong being rich monetarily (1 Tim. 6:16–18), but the Scriptures also speak of it as a potential curse and extreme burden if it is not used properly or with the right intention (1 Tim. 6:8–11).

Let us, as we begin to develop what spiritual identity really is, cease and desist from teaching or believing that this wonderful spiritual calling has anything to do with us or our bank account. If it did, then God would give all of us a financial windfall when we came to know Him, for he surely does not play favorites within His family.

Don't be discouraged if all of this so far is a bit difficult to understand. I want to lighten your load and possible confusion with this reminder: If these truths were culturally accepted and easily understood in the Christian community, there would be little reason for this book. Though the message of our spiritual identity is starting to get some needed attention in books, in churches, and in Christianity as a whole, we are sadly still at the "baby-step stage," and these truths face a long journey ahead to again become the main fabric of teaching in our churches.

> While walking through the forest one day, a man found a young eagle that had fallen out of its nest. He took it home and put it in his barnyard, where it soon learned to eat and behave like the chickens. One day a naturalist passed by the farm and asked why it was that the king of all birds should be confined to live in the barnyard with

the chickens. The farmer replied that since he had given it chicken feed and trained it to be a chicken, it had never learned to fly. Since it now behaved as the chickens, it was no longer an eagle.

"Still, it has the heart of an eagle," replied the naturalist, "and can surely be taught to fly." He lifted the eagle toward the sky and said, "You belong to the sky and not to the earth. Stretch forth your wings and fly." The eagle, however, was confused. He did not know who he was, and seeing the chickens eating their food, he jumped down to be with them again.

The naturalist took the bird to the roof of the house and urged him again, saying, "You are an eagle. Stretch forth your wings and fly." But the eagle was afraid of his unknown self and world and jumped down once more for the chicken food. Finally, the naturalist took the eagle out of the barnyard to a high mountain. There he held the king of the birds high above him and encouraged him again, saying, "You are an eagle. You belong to the sky. Stretch forth your wings and fly." The eagle looked around, back towards the barnyard and up to the sky. Then the naturalist lifted him straight towards the sun, and it happened that the eagle began to tremble. Slowly, he stretched his wings, and with a triumphant cry, soared away into the heavens.

It may be that the eagle still remembers the chickens with nostalgia. It may even be that he occasionally revisits the barnyard. But as far as anyone knows, he has never returned to lead the life of a chicken.[4] That

[4] "A Chicken or an Eagle," Theology News and Notes, October, 1976, quoted in Multnomah Message, Spring, 1993, p. 1.

is what we will try to develop in this book. You certainly are not what you should be in your spiritual life, but I want to remind you: If you are truly born-again of the Spirit and you know it, you are not what you used to be! **Don't miss that!** If you are in God's estimation an "eagle," then you could never be a chicken—and if you are not a chicken, then why live like you are? God has moved you out of the chicken coop, and He has graciously given you the wings and flight of a spiritual eagle. Beginning now, spread those wings and begin to soar. You can do it. God and I will help you!

Part I

Laying the Foundation and Order of Spiritual Identity

2

Laying the Only Proper Spiritual Foundation

"For no one can lay any foundation other than the one already laid, which is Jesus Christ."

—1 Corinthians 3:11 (NIV)

"So then you are no longer strangers and aliens, but you are fellow citizens with the saints and members of the household of God, built on the foundation of the apostles and prophets, Christ Jesus himself being the cornerstone, in whom the whole structure, being joined together, grows into a holy temple in the Lord."

—Ephesians 2:19–21 (ESV)

It's all about you.

Really, Chris? You read it right. When it comes to spiritual identity, the *focus* is on what God has done for *us*, not on what we can do *for* Him. Even more than what He does for us is the subject of what *we* are in Him. No, I am not proclaiming a "me-centered, egocentric gospel." I have not fallen into the deception of believing that man is the CEO in the inner workings of God's business and that his self-effort and accomplishments are what God gets great pleasure from. Nothing could be further from the truth.

There is little doubt that, according to the Scriptures, God is working all things out in the universe for His glory first and that He alone is to be first place in our lives (Eph. 1:11; Col. 1:15–21). Did you hear what I just said? So in that sense, absolutely everything in life and in our life is about Him first and predominantly! I got it. I get it. I know for real that everything starts with this bedrock belief of Scripture. I have, in fact, championed those beliefs most of my Christian life. But, listen: Knowing this truth plainly uncovers another life changing truth as well. Are you ready for this? Here it is:

God wants you and me to know that "we," as His beloved children, are the apple of His eye and what He says and feels about us matters most.

In his message *How to Build a Life That Lasts,* pastor Jack Graham[5] tells the story of how Bill Walton cut his hair and his beard and learned how to play basketball like few men before or since. Even until the day coach Wooden graduated to heaven, he would respectfully refer to him as "Coach Wooden," and every week, he would call Coach just to tell him how much he loved him. Wooden, you see, was much more

---

[5] Pastor Jack Graham, "Rock Solid: How to Build a Life That Lasts," *Preaching.com,* http://www.preaching.com/sermons/11548356/.

than a coach to his players. He became their father figure. Of the 188 or so players that he coached during his career, he knew the whereabouts of 172. Coach Wooden was committed to the basics. He taught his players the importance of building a solid foundation for success—in basketball and in life.

That is what the identity driven life embodies, and it is why our spiritual foundation is what really counts most in this life.

We must know that without a strong and reliable foundation, no building—or life, for that matter—will ultimately stand. What looks good to the naked eye is not always what it seems to be. If you ever had a chance to participate in coaching sports or lead a group in some capacity, you know full well the importance of teaching the "simple, elementary truths" to the people you are working with so that they can actually do what is being asked of them. **KISS** (Keep It Simple, Stupid) is a harsh but wise measurement for relating truth to others. This proper spiritual foundation is what people need all over the world, and it is what they are crying out for when you really begin to break down the human condition. People can accomplish a lot in life, and by all accounts, it looks like they are succeeding. Yet, if a proper spiritual foundation has not been laid and the old "life building" of their lives in time radically renovated, a personal crash and burn is inevitable: mark it down.

As we begin our journey together to discover all that God says about us, we must lay a proper biblical foundation that works. One that works when we are spiritually on the mountaintop as well as a foundation that works with the same power and effectiveness when we are at the end of our proverbial rope and our stress level is clearly off the chain. You and I were not made to live by one emotional experience after another or to live our lives with just a "tough it out" mentality. Christ, who is our life (Col. 3:4), remade us to live for so much more.

It is sad to say that many reading this book have come to the conclusion that the "abundant, overcoming life" Jesus talked about in John 10:10 is only reserved for heaven someday, not for the here and now. I have clearly observed that when we succumb to that "lie," we who call ourselves evangelical Christians tend to, sooner or later, settle into a second-rate spiritual existence, where trying our best is the best we can hope for.

Let me paint a picture that hopefully helps.

We Christians have learned the rotten art of stylishly dressing up our sinful, egotistical flesh in religious fashion that we perceive will be accepted by God and admired by others. We ignorantly have been deceived into believing that the best existence we can hope for on Earth is this torturous grind of "sinning and confessing, sinning and confessing, hoping to someday overcome the 'demons' within." Yet, when we settle into this kind of living, all we are really doing is fine-tuning the lifestyle of self-deception, and that is the worst kind of deception of all. We are left asking, "Is this really all there is, Lord?"

I love what the apostle Paul says to the Colossian believers who are going through this same struggle. In chapter 2, verses 6 and 7, the Amplified Version really breaks it down well:

As you have therefore received Christ, [even] Jesus the Lord, [so] walk (regulate your lives and conduct yourselves) in union with and conformity to Him. Have the roots [of your being] firmly and deeply planted [in Him, fixed and founded in Him], being continually built up in Him, becoming increasingly more confirmed and established in the faith. . . . (AMP)

Notice that our Christian experience needs to have "roots firmly and deeply planted, being continually built up in Him" [that is Christ]. I wonder how many of us can say, "That's me Chris; I can say with all honesty that I am aggressively and confidently moving in that direction!" I hope you can say that. Believe me, I do. But having spent over thirty years of my life teaching church folks, I can tell you that this "kind" of Christian is getting increasingly rarer. I wish I could say that I was jumping to a crazy, unfounded conclusion, but I don't believe I am. So the question is: Why is this true? Why do we not see in increasing numbers "fully devoted followers of Jesus Christ," especially in the Western world?

Think about it this way. Whenever we look at a home to purchase, we often are pulled in by the excellent decor of the home. Realtors call this "curbside appeal." Very often, it is the exterior and/or the interior design of the home and the way the house is laid out that really sells the home. Rarely, if ever, is the purchase contingent on a full knowledge of the house's foundation. I mean who ever asks when buying a house, "What is the condition of the foundation?"

Why? Because we assume that the foundation is secure. Yet there are countless stories about homes, bridges, and other massive structures whose poor engineering or substandard concrete work greatly compromised the quality of the structure, and in the end, catastrophe struck. But listen: no one knew the true condition of the foundation until a crisis stressed the building. Don't blow off what I just said. It is foundational for our study. What I am saying is this. The crisis *revealed* the quality of the foundation; it did not *cause* it.

Notice what author and pastor Tullian Tchividjian has to say about this: "Suffering exposes the foundation of your life." In other words, suffering will reveal the true source of our joy and identity. Tullian offers the following personal story to illustrate this profound truth:

> Seven years ago, after 41 years of marriage, my parents got divorced. It wasn't because of infidelity or abuse, physically or emotionally. My family and I still scratch our heads and wonder exactly what happened. Was it really a case of irreconcilable differences? I don't think that's possible for Christians because of the power of the gospel. It was an incredibly painful time for my siblings and me. We experienced a happy, healthy, loving home growing up. We had remarkable parents, and they provided the stability we needed as children. I don't know what it's like for a mom and dad to go through a divorce while their children are young. All I know is that it's weird to watch your parents' divorce in the stage of life where you have to explain it to your own kids.

The Bible states clearly that God hates divorce. It grieves his heart. There was nothing about my parents' divorce that seemed redemptive. I couldn't understand why God allowed it to happen. I was struggling with the whole situation, not simply because I was sad that my mom and dad apparently could not keep the promises they made to one another 41 years earlier, but because part of my identity was wrapped up in being the son of my parents. I felt important because of their standing in society. My mom and dad were remarkable citizens and church people. Their reputation made me feel significant. I realized years later that much of the devastation I had experienced was due to the fact that I had idolized my parents and their reputation.

Tullian concludes: "If the foundation of your happiness is your vocation, your relationships, or your money, then suffering takes your source of joy away from you. But if your ultimate value in life is God, then suffering drives you closer to your source of joy—God."[6]
This is what Jesus meant when he reminded the crowds of his day:

I will show you what he is like who comes to me and hears my words and puts them into practice. He is like a man building a house, who dug down deep and laid the foundation on rock. When a

---

[6] Tullian Tchividjian, "Job: Center Stage," as quoted in "Sermons," *Preaching Today*, http://www.preachingtoday. com/sermons/sermons/2012/may/jobcenterstage. html?start=8.

flood came, the torrent struck that house but
could not shake it, because it was well built.
(Luke 6:47–48, NIV)

In Jesus' day, the foundations of buildings were
constructed block by block. That is a great model
on which to build our new life. Many believers in
Jesus try to live life without this firm, solid spiritual
foundation. It's not on purpose. None of us go
through life with a desire to crumble under life's
load. I just don't think it occurs to us that our lives
may, just may, be built on shifting, soft sand. So,
when a powerful storm hits home, we run the risk
of being spiritually exposed and knocked off center
for some time. We often see Christianity as a "cure
all" to our past life and hurts and believe that just
"adding Christian stuff" to our lives will alleviate
most of our outer problems and inner turmoil. We
look great and strong to the unskilled spiritual eye,
but this seeming "together life" is one heavy storm
away from spiritual disaster. It is then that our faith
reveals its true temperature, and if our foundation
is unreliable, we often grow bitter and disappointed
with God. Nothing else shows the "faith level" of a
person more honestly than during these days. It is
important for us to know that God very often allows
the storms of life to drench us so *we* can see where
our faith level really is. He already knows where it is,
but He wants us to face the music as well. It is easier
to serve Christ when all is well, but the foundation
of our life may not be challenged in those days.
The challenge and growth opportunities are often
revealed when the pressure on our foundation is

the greatest. That is why our spiritual foundation is what, at the end of the day, really counts most.

When you study the Bible and you start to "connect the dots" of verses that partner with other verses, the phrase "the rock" describes that we must build our life on—*Jesus Christ*. This "rock" is identified descriptively in 1 Corinthians 10:4 as Christ Himself. His sinless personal life and what He accomplished for us in his death and resurrection is that foundation that we must build our lives on. Religion, denominationalism, or even a neat set of creeds and beliefs are not enough to bear under life's tremendous weight. It never was and it isn't going to change anytime soon.

It is interesting to note that when Hebrews 12 tells us that we are in a "race," the word for race in the Greek language (the language the Newer Testament was written in) is the word *agon*, in which we get the English word "agony." That's interesting. Here's what that says to me: God is not afraid to shoot straight with us about how hard life can be. It is admittedly agonizing to go through this fallen world on our way to our real home. God keeps it real so we do not expect something that is never promised. He never paints (and we shouldn't either) a fairyland mural about life in this fallen, broken world. Life is hard, but thankfully, God is always good. Life is hard, yes, but the good news is biblical Christianity projects realism through and through. It is encouraging to know that while life is difficult, God can be fully trusted to be our strength in life's low points.

So we can say that it is more than just a "suggestion" to know and have Jesus as our sure and secure foundation. Without Him, we are, at some point, going to fall or crumble. Let me say that again. Jesus *has* to be our firm and secure foundation or we, at some point, are going to crumble. That is not my opinion. It is an eternal truth that cannot be effectively disputed. I am finding more and more that He is more than enough for my life and my desire for godly living. We should not be surprised at that, because that is exactly what the apostle Peter said in his second letter (2 Pet. 1:3-4). When you realize that Jesus is more than enough, your Christian life will radically begin to change, and others will notice the change.

As we look closer at the importance of laying a proper spiritual foundation, there are a series of biblical verses that tie this thought together. When I was a new convert, I wish I had been told what I am about to tell you. It would have saved me a lot of heartache and internal struggle early on.

Have you ever thought that the Christian life is so darn difficult? That there seem to be some major puzzle pieces missing from your board? That what God demands from you doesn't seem to be fair or even possible to pull off? I have asked that question a lot over the years, and I have heard countless others ask the same question, but I can honestly and humbly say that I do not ask that question anymore . . . and I haven't for a long time. Now, please don't read into my words some sort of an "I'm better than you" attitude. That's not my point or feeling at all. I am acutely aware of how desperate I am without Christ in my life. Believe me.

My point is really a simple one, and I don't want you to miss it: I have and am discovering more and more the desire of Christ for my Christian living. His desire is He longs for me to be stable and confident in my walk in Him. This kind of life is not a fairy tale or reserved for just the religious types in our world. The offer, opportunity, and challenge are to any and all who would crawl in childlike faith to Christ. He doesn't play favorites like we often do.

Let me put it in these terms:

For me, being a Christian for over thirty years has little to do with (note I didn't say nothing) *understanding* how to live the Christian life. You know how I know this? Because I know a lot of Christians that have been in the family longer than I who are still "babies" and spiritually shaky on their feet when it comes to the things of God.

For me, this understanding has not come from faithfully reading my Bible or maintaining a faithful "quiet time." You know how I know this? Because there are countless believers who seem to consistently practice these disciplines really well that are, if truth be told, out of their minds spiritually and always seem to be on the brink of spiritual collapse.

For me, I have discovered it does not come from being in the right church or reading from the "right version of the Bible" or from knowing all the right people in Christendom. You know how I know this? Because so many of us have rode these sacred cows, and it has not delivered to us what we are searching for deep on the inside. *External* hope to solve the crimes of our heart is fruitless when it comes right down to it. So, where do spiritual stability and a proper spiritual foundation come from? We will investigate that in a bit, but let me prove to you why God and His Son, Jesus, desire that we be spiritually stable, spiritually mature, and spiritually deep.

Try These Verses on for Size . . .

The following verses describe God's desire for **all** of His children.

Colossians 1:28 (NIV)

"We proclaim him [Christ], admonishing and teaching everyone with all wisdom, so that we may present everyone perfect in Christ."

The word "perfect" in verse 28 is an interesting word in the Greek language. It means to be complete or mature. It conveys the idea of being well-rounded or stable. Someone wrote that one of the great goals of Christian teaching is seen in this verse, and I have to agree. It is actually one of my life verses as it relates to my immense privilege of serving in pastoral ministry.

Ephesians 4:11–14 (NIV)

It was he who gave some to be apostles, some to be prophets, some to be evangelists, and some to be pastors and teachers, to prepare God's people for works of service, so that the body of Christ may be built up until we all reach unity in the faith and in the knowledge of the Son of God and become mature, attaining to the whole measure of the fullness of Christ. Then we will no longer be infants, tossed back and forth by the waves, and blown here and there by every wind of teaching and by the cunning and craftiness of men in their deceitful scheming.

These verses are ripe with serious implications. Paul says that the goal of every truly called spiritual leader in the church is twofold.

First, they are to live their lives and ministry in such a way that God's people will be prepared for serving Christ in the culture so the church may grow numerically and spiritually (4:12–13). Wow! That really puts the responsibilities of leaders and the role of parish members in proper perspective.

The second goal of every leader from God's perspective is to conduct their ministry so that every Christian can become spiritually strong and stable in their walk of faith. "No longer infants" implies that God longs to see us all grow up and stand on our own two feet spiritually. That is God's normal for every Christian. A child is a true child not because he acts like one, but because he *is* one. A teen or twentysomething can act like a child at times, but they can never truly be one. There is an expectation that when we leave childhood, everyone will notice. At least that is the natural expectation.

Hebrews 5:13–14 (NLT)

For someone who lives on milk is still an infant and doesn't know how to do what is right. Solid food is for those who are mature, who, through training, have the skill to recognize the difference between right and wrong.

What is God saying here? Simply that His desire for "baby Christians" is to start to walk, then firmly stand, and then, consistently run! God did not design a process that would see His children reborn spiritually and then not grow or mature in their faith. As we said earlier, such a process would be abnormal and unhealthy. It is interesting that the writer of Hebrews says that the one who lives on milk "doesn't know how to do what is right." Yet, those who are mature can endure "solid food," and the assumption is that they know how to make good decisions that honor God. God wants all of us to grow up, and that only can happen if we don't skip the crawling and standing part. If we get this discipline down, then we can run to win the race that God has set for us.

Many Christians are running their fool heads off, serving God with all their might, but sooner or later, they are going to collapse in a pile of spiritual perspiration. Why? Because the spiritual foundation of their Christian life that has been laid has not been properly built upon. The building that houses their man- centered life is quickly slipping into a sea of depression and defeat. And that breaks the heart of God. Something has to give.

The Leaning Tower of Pisa in Italy has recently been shored up. It's a good thing. Without this process, it was on its way to certain collapse. Scientists traveled yearly to measure the building's slow descent. They reported that the 179-foot tower moved about one-twentieth of an inch a year, and most recently was more than 17 feet out of whack. Years ago, the Italian government estimated that by the year 2007, the 810-year-old tower would have leaned too far and would collapse onto a nearby restaurant. Though because of an intervention this did not happen, it would have happened someday, and the devastation would have been significant. It is interesting that the word "pisa" means "marshy land," which gives us some clue as to why the tower began to lean even before it was completed. Also, just for the record and for our understanding, its foundation is only 10 feet deep. That is more than coincidental. The absence of a deep foundation is always going to be a problem . . . and a potential nightmare in life and in our Christian lives.

As we lay the foundation of this book, we need to again be reminded of how important the elementary principles of Scripture are. The foundation of our Christian life must be sure and deep. A surface foundation simply won't stand. When God wants to grow a mushroom, He does not root this plant very deep at all. When He wants to grow an oak, He runs the roots of this tree deeply into the soil so it can endure any storm that comes along. As God's own, we are *not* mushrooms. The Bible says we are "oaks of righteousness," and God is building us into people that can stand up against the greatest of tragedy. You need to know that this "spiritual root system" is effectively fertilized by our understanding and living out our identity in Christ. And it is seen more clearly by understanding God's divine teaching order in the New Testament.

That is our subject on our next stop. Keep in mind, though: *We're just getting warmed up!*

3

God's Order in the Newer Testament (Part 1)

"Not only do we not know God except through Jesus Christ; we do not even know ourselves except through Jesus Christ."

—Blaise Pascal[7]

"The truth about our spiritual identity in Christ is not contained in one verse or another, but due to its beauty and complexity, is interwoven throughout the New Testament."

—Larry Silver[8]

---

[7] "Inspirational Quotes," *Beliefnet,* http://www.beliefnet.com/Quotes/Evangelical/B/Blaise-Pascal/Not-Only-Do-We-Not-Know-God-Except-Through-Jesus-C.aspx. Blaise Pascal (1623–1662) was a French mathematician, physicist and Christian philosopher.

[8] Larry Silver, *Spiritual Identity* (Mustang, OK: Tate Publishing & Enterprises, 2007), 16.

Without spiritual order in our lives, we are helplessly plotting through life hoping to land somewhere.

A man limps into a hospital to have his foot X-rayed and is asked to wait for the results. Sometime later, an orderly appears and hands the man a large pill. As he's handed the pill, a mother with a small child in need of immediate attention enters, and the orderly disappears with the new patient.

The man with the foot problem hobbles over to get a glass of water, swallows the pill, and sits down to wait. Sometime later, the orderly reappears bringing a bucket of water to the man with the limp.

"Okay," he said, "Let's drop the pill in this bucket and soak your foot for a while."

Our own behaviors can circumvent the very cure we need.[9]

Never has this story been more true than when we talk about "God's order or prescription" for mankind in general and for His children in particular.

Don Matzat, in his extremely insightful book *Christ Esteem: Where the Search for Self-Esteem Ends,* writes these words.

It is my purpose to demonstrate that a relationship with the person of Jesus Christ more than adequately solves the identity crisis of this generation and brings meaning and

[9] "Curing Church Conflict-2" *Sermon Central,* http://www.sermoncentral.com/sermons/curing-church-conflict-2-byron-sherman-sermon-on-conflict-182835.asp.

fulfillment of life[10] . . . in addition to being our righteousness, Jesus Christ is also our identity, our life, our fulfillment, our pride, our hope, our peace, our joy, and our ultimate worth[11] . . . our new identity and life is determined by the historical redeeming work of Jesus Christ[12] . . . The New Testament directive to find our identity and life in Christ Jesus is not a simplistic solution. It is profound."[13]

Matzat's last phrase is what I want to hitchhike on in this chapter because for some time now, I have believed what Matzat believes. Why is what he says so profound, and why is his premise not more widely used as a solution to the spiritual condition of all of us? Let's look hard at that question.

In this chapter, we will see how God, in His infinite wisdom, has ordered the Newer Testament in relation to its teaching. From Jesus in the gospels to Peter's final two epistles and even in the apostle John's letters, including the Revelation Of Jesus Christ, the message of our spiritual identity always comes before the message of our spiritual purpose. *Always!* It is so important that we see not only the truth of this but also why this is the case. God is a God of order, and if we fail to follow His divine order, we will not receive either the message He wants to relay correctly, or even

---

[10] Don Matzat, *Christ Esteem: Where the Search for Self-Esteem Ends* (Eugene, OR: Harvest House, 1990), 11.

[11] Ibid., 31.

[12] Ibid., 75.

[13] Ibid., 192.

more soberly, we will not be able to follow His message in its *intended* form. The result will be us living lives of quiet desperation rather than an abundant life rooted in Christ. So it is not about whether identity is more important than purpose. They are both vitally important. It is just about the order and I think you would agree—His order stands supreme!

"The New Testament directive," as Matzat puts it, has been largely overlooked by the church for a long time. It has somehow been put on the shelf of the minds of the Christian populace for many decades now. Let me propose why I believe this is the case.

When you look at the Christian books that were being authored seventy to one hundred years ago or more, you notice one obvious thing—these books were especially centered on the Christian life and on how to walk this "Christ life" out. Writers named J. Hudson Taylor, Andrew Murray, Ruth Paxson, Watchman Nee, Ian Thomas, Norman Grubb, Charles Trumbell, William Newell, Jessie Penn-Lewis, F. J. Huegel, and Evan Hopkins were writers who explained the Christian life in an orderly and simple manner. I can just imagine what many of you are thinking right now: "Who *are* these people? Eldredge, I know; Chan, I know; Meyer, I know; Osteen, I know; but who are these others you mention?" They were simply men and women of another time who believed that the "foundation" of our identity in Christ was what God's people needed to rest on if they were ever going to be powerfully used by God. Don't yawn over that last statement. It will bring into focus what we are going to discuss the next few minutes.

So what has actually happened in the last seventy-five years or so in the Christian church and particularly the Christian writing market?

What Has Happened to the Foundations?

Now I know that some will criticize me for this seemingly broad brush explanation of where we have been and what we have become as a society and the church. I can appreciate that, but my only logical response would be: do you have a better overall explanation of why we are today where we are as the body of Christ?

It has been pointed out by a few wise churchologists that around sixty or seventy years ago, around the time when World War II was ending and the sexual revolution of the late 50s and 60s was in its infancy, the American family was in deep trouble. The length and scope of the war and the widespread absence of fathers in the home, as well as the fast moving erosion of sexual standards in society, caused the deep "felt need" in America's churches to shift. This shift took place when the emphasis of discipleship and evangelism gave way to feverishly rescuing the troubled family and saving failing marriages. Christian colleges known for their deep commitment to teaching and training God's people in the foundations of the faith slowly began to adopt policies and procedures that catered more to cultural, pragmatic thinking. Timeless biblical principles that the early church introduced were slowly but steadily replaced with human philosophy and pop psychology. There was a growing belief in religious circles that the answer to the social ills of the day could not be fully addressed by the standards of Scripture.

The church at large began to adopt more "professional help" to handle the ambush of family breakdown. In short, the truths of Christ and the elementary principles of the faith began to be exchanged with faulty, man-centered thinking with still a "little Jesus" thrown in. This shift centered on "self" and man's ability to overcome the temptations they faced, albeit with "God's help." Christ-centered writing was replaced with self-help, psychological material that encompassed neat little formulas to get with the program. The church and then the family began to offer man-made ideologies to slow the rising tide of the spiritual tsunami that visited the shores of family life. In our approach to Christian living, the *vertical* (God to us) slowly began to be replaced with the *horizontal* (man to man). How we lived out our spousal and parenting roles and even the way we approached ministry was beginning to travel down some shaky, unproven trails, and that is essentially where we have been these many years. The result is that we in the Western world are up to our necks in "flesh and self," and where self is king, Christ is conspicuously absent. That is just keeping it real, my friend. God will not share His glory with another! That is the road that we have run on for the last half century or more, especially in America, and the corresponding results from it have left us wildly adrift and sinking fast!

You may be asking at this point—So *what*, Chris? Does all this really matter today, and does it matter personally? What can we do about it anyway?

Solomon asked the same question almost three thousand years ago when he said, "If the foundations

be destroyed, what can the righteous do?" Well, for
starters, we must begin to seriously look to "rebuild
the foundations" if we are ever going to see deep
spiritual revival sweep across our shores again. The
shaky and shifting sand we are on is giving way in
growing ways, and if Christianity is to thrive again
and not just survive until Jesus returns, the winds of
deep spiritual change must blow in and blow in *fast*!

God's Order in the Newer Testament

The great eighteenth century poet Alexander Pope
once wrote, "Order is heaven's first law."[14] I agree
with him. God is indeed a God of order. There is no
legitimate argument about that.

So what is God's order in the New Testament as it
relates to our new identity in Christ?

To begin with, we must understand (and Jesus made
it clear) that what happens *in* us is of far more value than
what happens *to* us or even comes *from* us. Put another
way, what God has done in us and what He chooses to
do through us is to be valued most by us. *Why?* Simply
because if the source of our strength and success is
rooted in Christ, then He will get all the glory and credit
he rightfully deserves, and that is good news for us.

Jesus' Two Cents about Spiritual Identity

In Luke chapter 10, verse 1, Luke records this: "The
Lord now chose seventy-two other disciples and sent
them ahead in pairs to all the towns and places he

---

[14] "Alexander Pope Quotes," *BrainyQuote,* http://www.brainy-
quote.com/quotes/quotes/a/alexanderp143063.html.

planned to visit" (NLT). Jesus gives them instructions about what they should say and do "out in the field" and they would then report back to him. When they return, Luke paints this scene:

> When the seventy-two disciples returned, they joyfully reported to him, "Lord, even the demons obey us when we use your name!" "Yes," he told them, "I saw Satan fall from heaven like lightning! Look, I have given you authority over all the power of the enemy and you can walk among snakes and scorpions and crush them. Nothing will injure you. **But don't rejoice because evil spirits obey you; rejoice because your names are registered in heaven**. (NLT; emphasis mine)

Did you catch that last phrase in verse 20? It is easy to pass right over it and miss Jesus' point. I want you to see that what the Savior says underscores "God's Order in the New Testament" with an exclamation point! What he says is the foundation that the apostle Paul and Peter will later build on as they communicate to us God's divine order for Christian living. So what I am going to say in this chapter is extremely relevant to the case I am building.

In this story, Jesus was saying who you are is of far greater value than what you do. "Lord, even the demons obey us when we use your name" was the bragimony of the seventy-two. Jesus responds by saying (in verse 17–18) that being proud of what we have accomplished is comparable to the pride that Satan possessed when he got his walking papers in heaven. It is, by all accounts, very strong language. Jesus reminds them that He has given them all that they need to do His work, but verse 20 reminds them "don't rejoice because evil spirits obey you. . . ." Say *what*, Jesus? Let's review: Jesus sends them out to minister in His name, and when they come back, they are stoked—but it seems that they are stoked about the wrong thing. How do I know that? Because Jesus rebukes them for what they thought was most important. He uses the words, "Don't rejoice. . . ." I want you to see that they were all worked up about what *they* had been able to accomplish, but they were unmoved by the eternal truth that their names were recorded in heaven. After all, that privilege is not reserved for most of creation.

Let me share some insights from this story so you can better understand the Holy Spirit's purpose in all this.

First, who we are as children of God is far more valuable than what we can do as children of God.

Second, spiritual pride is ours if we think our works and what comes from them is what serving Christ is all about.

Third, our spiritual position as a child of God is what God is interested in most, and our condition (*what* we are as a result of *who* we are) is an outflow of that spiritual position. Don't miss that. We will build on this more in a moment.

Lastly, God's Order for the New Testament is seen clearly in the words of Jesus: our joy first and foremost comes from a proper understanding of who we are and where we are going.

Paul's Letter Develops
This New Testament Order

In his classic work on Paul's letter to the Romans, William R. Newell wrote:

> Paul does not ask a thing of the saints in the first three chapters of Ephesians but just to listen while he proclaims that wondrous series of great and eternal facts concerning them; and not until he has completed this catalogue of realities about them does he ask them to do anything at all! And when he does open his plea for their high walk as saints, everything is based on the revelation before given the facts of their high character and destiny as saints: "I therefore ... beseech you that ye walk worthy of the vocation wherewith ye are called" (Eph. 4:1). Let us cease laying down to the saints long lists of "conditions" of entering into the blessed life in Christ; and instead, as the primal preparation for leading them into the experience of this life, show them what their position, possessions, and privileges in Christ already are. **Thus shall we truly work with the Holy Spirit, and thus shall we have more and much more abiding fruit of our labors among the people of God** (emphasis mine)."[15]

Those last words from Newell sum up what I am trying to say. If you don't see the order, then the rest of the chapters will make little impact in your life. Newell believed (as I do) that when we understand

[15] William Newell, *Romans: Verse by Verse*, (Grand Rapids, MI: Kregel, 1994), n.p.

God's order as it relates to who we are as a child of God, then "we truly work with the Holy Spirit," and as God's people, we will be much more effective in working His kingdom plan. Isn't "spiritual effectiveness" what it's all about at the end of the day?

Providentially, God led Paul especially to divide his letters into two sections. The first part is what we have come to call "doctrinal." The second half of his letters is what is called the "practical" section, which is a simply a plea to live out what we know about our relationship in Christ. We cannot gloss over (and we have, as the church) the doctrinal sections of Scripture and just jump headlong in to the practical sections. That mistake has been one of the major reasons for a weak church in the last half century.

4

God's Order in the Newer Testament (Part 2)

Without spiritual order in our lives, we are helplessly plotting through life hoping to land somewhere.

I love what Bill Hull writes in his book *The Disciple-Making Church*. With regard to the order of character and duty, he says:

> Orthopraxy (right practice) is always derived from orthodoxy (right doctrine). Those who say, "Let's not be doctrinal; let's be practical," amuse me, because I find it impossible to be practical without being doctrinal. Doctrine drives practice. Paul's applications are helpful because they grow out of a theological base. Modern church thinkers have increasingly lost sight of this truth. Contemporary theology often allows

application to grow from pragmatism and the social sciences.[16]

Well said, Bill.

Let me walk you through the New Testament beginning with Romans and show you the "divine order" of teaching as it relates to our Christian life, and in particular, to what I call the identity driven life. You ready for this? It is truly beautiful.

Romans

In chapter 1, verses 1 through 7, the apostle Paul reminds the Romans of their "spiritual calling" first before anything else! He says you are these "who are called to belong to Jesus Christ. To all in Rome who are loved by God and called to be his holy people." Notice Paul uses the word "called" twice. We cannot miss its value. To be called by God is to be singled out by God and chosen by Him to be one of His own. There is nothing we can do to be called, and there is nothing we can do to stay called. It is all by God's free grace, and it is because we are "loved by God." We are called to belong to Jesus Christ. That is our true spiritual identity. Once we belonged to the kingdom of Satan; now we belong to the King over Satan (Col. 1:12–13).

Someone might say, "OK, got it, but what does that have to do with what we are talking about?" It has everything to do with it. Before the apostle gets into man's true fallen condition without God (chapters

---

[16] Bill Hull, *The Disciple-Making Church*, updated ed. (Ada, MI: Baker Books, 2010), 158.

1–5), he lets the Romans believers know that what they used to be is not what they are now. They have had a change of identity, of person, of purpose, and of destiny. If you outline Romans, you will again see God's divine order. *Who we are is first. What we do flows from knowing who we are.*

I & 2 Corinthians

Paul lays out these two letters similar to Romans. In the first chapter, Paul reminds these believers in Corinth of who they are far before they are asked to perform any works. Question; in fact, the same question I asked in chapter 1 when we were talking about "saints":

Again, who were the most fleshly, misguided, immature believers in the New Testament? And the answer: the Corinthians. As we pointed out earlier, this church had more problems than a mathematician. But enter the order of God and the identity message, and now we're talking. Again, the Amplified version sums up verses 1 and 2 of chapter 1 rather well.

Paul, summoned by the will and purpose of God to be an apostle (special messenger) of Christ Jesus, and our brother Sosthenes, To the church (assembly) of God which is in Corinth, to those consecrated and purified and made holy in Christ Jesus, [who are] selected and called to be saints (God's people), together with all those who in any place call upon and give honor to the name of our Lord Jesus Christ, both their Lord and ours. (NLT)

There it is again. "To the church, consecrated and purified and made holy in Christ, who are selected and called to be saints. ..." They certainly hadn't lived up to this place in God's family. They certainly weren't acting like they were God's kids. But before Paul breaks out the paddle and deals out the time-out sessions, he reminds them of their spiritual position, which is rooted in God's grace and not in their goodness.

Notice the divine order again: who we are in Christ is first. What we do flows from knowing who we are. What the Corinthians were doing was not reflective of who they were. In the second letter in verse 1, Paul writes, "I am writing to God's church in Corinth and to all of his holy people throughout Greece. . . ." Again, he is reminding them of who they are before he gives them a to do list.

Galatians

In Galatians, it is a little harder to see this divine order, but it is there, for sure. It is especially highlighted in chapter 2, verses 19 through 21.

> For when I tried to keep the law, it condemned me. So I died to the law, I stopped trying to meet all its requirements so that I might live for God. My old self has been crucified with Christ. It is no longer I who live, but Christ lives in me. So I live in this earthly body by trusting in the Son of God, who loved me and gave himself for me. I do not treat the grace of God as meaningless. For if keeping the law could make us right with God, then there was no need for Christ to die. (NLT)

Verse 20 is a key verse concerning our "identity" in Christ. We are identified with Christ in His death and resurrection, so much so that the life we live now is Christ and not us (Col. 3:4). In chapters 3 through 6, Paul's argument to the spiritual legalists who were infiltrating the ranks of believers there as well is simply this: know who you are in Christ and start living accordingly. The divine order remains the same as in Romans and the two recorded letters to the Corinthians.

Ephesians

This letter, like Romans, neatly reveals the divine order for Christian living. In fact, I dare say it is possibly clearer than the great epistle of Romans. In Ephesians 1–3, Paul shares with the believers the great spiritual wealth they enjoy in Christ. He reminds them in many different ways that they are chosen and called of God, selected in Jesus, and sealed by the Holy Spirit—all because of God's amazing, undeserved grace. Paul does not ask the Ephesian saints to do anything or become anything until he first reminds them of whom they are—and why doing the works of Christ must spring from knowing and resting in whom they are, which is the work of Christ. To put it another way, our doing *for* Christ must flow from our being *in* Christ.

This divine order is best seen in chapter 2, verse 10, where Paul writes, "For we are God's masterpiece. He has created us anew in Christ Jesus, so we can do the good things he planned for us long ago" (NLT). Notice the order: Who we are. What we are to do based on who we are. Christ's work first. Our work follows after.

Then, in chapter 4, verse 1, Paul transitions from basking in who the Ephesian Christians are in Christ to what they must do to live out their divine calling. "I therefore, a prisoner for the Lord, urge you to walk in a manner worthy of the calling to which you have been called" (ESV).

Notice the order: walk (do) as you have been called (be) in Christ. Paul believed, as I do, that service and works for Christ is a natural (really, supernatural) response to the work of Christ in our lives.

Colossians

In Paul's letter to the believers in the town of Colossae, the letter can be cut into two parts: (there's a surprise, right?) Chapters 1 *and* 2—doctrinal and foundational truths that identify us in Jesus Christ. Chapters 3 *and* 4—which primarily encourage the believers there to live out what they have come to know, and be in Christ. Time will not permit me to develop this divine order more fully, but if you study the letter closely, you will see this unmistakable order. This order of teaching was effectively engraved by the Holy Spirit in Paul's letters, and it must be a distinguishable mark in our teaching as well.

I agree totally with writer Neil Anderson when he writes, "It is my firm belief that if we fully appropriated the first half of Paul's epistles, which establish us in Christ, we would naturally (or supernaturally) live the second half." That really is the key message order of Paul in his letters.

I won't bore you with the details of this divine order beginning in Philippians and running through the Pastoral Epistles, but the order is even there, though, I admit, it is not as clearly laid out.

What Say You, Peter?

Paul, without question, effectively painted the "divine order" portrait that we need to see as Christians. We have seen that clearly. So did the apostle Peter.

Right out of the gate, Peter apparently picks up where Paul leaves off. Notice his words in chapter 1 of First Peter, verses 1 and 2:

> Peter, an apostle of Jesus Christ, To God's elect, exiles scattered throughout the provinces of Pontus, Galatia, Cappadocia, Asia and Bithynia, who have been chosen according to the foreknowledge of God the Father, through the sanctifying work of the Spirit, to be obedient to Jesus Christ and sprinkled with his blood: Grace and peace be yours in abundance. (NIV)

Check out the language Peter uses. "God's chosen people, foreigners, chose you long ago, has made you holy." And then the Holy Spirit, the author of Scripture, adds these words, "As a result. . . ." As a result of *what*, Peter? As a result of God's gracious work in them, "they have obeyed him. . . ." Here it is again. Who we are motivates what we do. I want you to know that obedience is the supernatural response to understanding the call of God on our lives. Once again, we are reminded that being always comes before doing.

In verses 3 through 12, Peter tells the believers more about their identity in Christ; in verses 13 through 16, he says that who they are must motivate a service for Christ that reflects holiness.

Peter's plea is a simple one: live out who you are. He does not tell them to live their Christian life out to become a child of God or an accepted member of God's household. That would "be out of order"! Read the rest of 1 Peter with this in mind, and you will see more of this begin to appear in a most beautiful way.

In his second letter, once again, he follows God's order of living when he writes in chapter 1, verse 3,

> His divine power has given us everything we need for a godly life through our knowledge of him who called us by his own glory and goodness. Through these he has given us his very great and precious promises, so that through them you may participate in the divine nature, having escaped the corruption in the world caused by evil desires. (NIV)

Let me sum these verses up. God has given us, on the front end, everything we need to live godly lives. That "everything" has to be primarily the message of who we are in Christ, or what we have come to call our "identity in Christ." Everything that we do in the power and in the name of Jesus flows from these foundational truths, or what Peter calls, "great and precious promises." God's word is swarming with principles that teach us to walk in Christ. Only then does Peter launch off into what the Christians he is writing to should be concentrating on in their walk. In verses 5 through 11, watch the order:

> For this very reason, make every effort to add to your faith goodness; and to goodness, knowledge; and to knowledge, self-control; and to self-control, perseverance; and to perseverance, godliness; and to godliness, mutual affection; and to mutual affection, love. For if you possess these qualities in increasing measure, they will keep you from being ineffective and unproductive in your knowledge of our Lord Jesus Christ. But whoever does not have them is nearsighted and blind, forgetting that they have been cleansed from their past sins.

> Therefore, my brothers and sisters, make every effort to confirm your calling and election. For if you do these things, you will never stumble, and you will receive a rich welcome into the eternal kingdom of our Lord and Savior Jesus Christ. (NIV)

In view of all this (verses 1–4), Peter says "make every effort to respond to God's promises." Not for nothing, but the divine order is alive and well, according to Peter. Didn't want you to doubt that at all!

Even the Apostle John Weighs In

The last heavy hitter in the New Testament is, of course, John the apostle. Many Bible scholars, and certainly tradition, uphold that he was the last original apostle to die and the only apostle to die from natural causes.

In the last book or letter in the collection of divine Scripture, the Revelation of Jesus Christ (better known as the book of Revelation), even *there*, in its opening words, John spells out God's divine order for Christian living. As if he had a meeting with Paul and Peter to compare notes, John spells out in the first chapter the need to see the great things that God has done for His church because of the work of His Son. Now keep in mind that John's Revelation is a treatise about Jesus Christ and His complete rule and reign over everything in the universe. It is *not* a book that extols Christian character or Christian living, by any means. It is not meant to. It is a book that unravels the work of God in the earth in the closing days of history and the divine emphasis on Jesus Christ as the main attraction throughout.

Yet, John, through the Spirit's leading, can't help himself being the apostle of love when he writes this in chapter 1, verses 4–6,

> John to the seven churches that are in Asia: Grace to you and peace from him who is and who was and who is to come, and from the seven spirits who are before his throne, and from Jesus Christ the faithful witness, the firstborn of the dead, and the ruler of kings on earth. To him who loves us and has freed us from our sins by his blood and made us a kingdom, priests to his God and Father, to him be glory and dominion forever and ever. Amen. (ESV)

He reminds those who are (in John's estimation at that time) about to deal with the great challenges that will visit the earth and their lives, the truth of who they are in Christ. Verse 5 encourages us with this: "To Him [Christ] who loves us and washed us from our sins and made us kings and priests. . . ." Yes, even John the apostle, in the last recorded words of the New Testament, weighs in on this vital teaching. Amazing, isn't it? But it is just like our God to give us a spiritual GPS even to the end that provides us the right way home.

As we close this chapter, I hope that you are beginning to assemble the puzzle pieces together in preparation for where we are going with all this. The journey is just beginning, and we have a lot of twists and turns to cover in this obstacle course.

Your greatest challenge as you read this book is to stay the course. Deal with the pain that God brings to the surface. Refuse to believe the lies of the enemy any longer. With that in mind, let's read on, shall we?

5

What Really Happened at Your Salvation?

"Salvation is the exchange of all that we are for all that He is."

—John MacArthur[17]

"All heaven is interested in the cross of Christ, all hell terribly afraid of it, while men are the only beings who more or less ignore its meaning.

—Oswald Chambers[18]

If all you know about your spiritual conversion policy is that you have fire insurance, then you better add to the policy a real promise of security.

---

[17] John MacArthur, *Matthew 1–7* (Chicago: Moody, 1985), 453.
[18] Oswald Chambers, *My Utmost for His Highest* (New York: Dodd Mead & Co., 1935; renewed by the Oswald Chambers Publications Assn., Ltd., 1963), n.p.

A humorous story is told of a baseball manager who decided to play a rookie in right field one day. The regular fielder wasn't happy about it and loudly makes it known from the bench that it was a big mistake to play the kid.

As it turned out, the rookie was so nervous that he messed up big-time. He made a couple of errors and misjudged several other fly balls that should have been called errors. Each time he messed up, the veteran complained loudly from the bench.

Finally, late in the game, the manager replaced the rookie with the veteran, mostly to shut the veteran up. Not long after, the veteran mishandled the first ball hit to him for an error. As he came off the field at the end of the inning, everyone on the bench got very quiet so they could hear what he would say.

The manager was waiting for the veteran, but before the manager could address the man, the veteran ballplayer slammed his glove down in disgust and said, "Skipper, that kid has right field so messed up nobody can play it."

This illustrates in a small way the challenge of understanding what eternal salvation really is all about. It is simple in its message, but we earthlings love to complicate it.

When I first came to know the Lord, I was like most everyone else—happy, and at the same time, completely clueless! I knew something significant had happened, but what, I couldn't tell you. I can remember asking Christ to save me from my sins one afternoon and then getting up and going about my night seemingly unaffected. Yet, in the weeks that followed, I began to have new affections and desires that could best be described as "foreign." One of the first things that I and others noticed is that my speech was severely sanitized almost overnight. If you knew me, you would probably say that I was outwardly a nice kid. But if the truth be told (*and I plan to tell it*), I was really angry on the inside. I hated myself, and because of that, I was short on patience with others. My speech was not only offensive, but extremely hurtful. But with the wave of His supernatural wand, Christ delivered me from my favorite pastime: verbally assassinating others. I noticed right away that the anger in my heart was beginning to dissolve, and Jesus' love was flooding in! It has now been over three decades since Christ met me where I was, and it has truly made all the difference.

In this chapter, I want to look deeply into this life we call "the Christian life." What really happened at your salvation? You may not have had the same experience as I did, but what exactly did Christ do for *you* when He saved you from your sin and self?

Sociologists have a theory called "the looking-glass self." It in essence says that you become what the most important person in your life (wife, father, boss, etc.) thinks you are. That's interesting! How would your life change if you truly believed the Bible's astounding words concerning God's love for you? If you and I simply and fearlessly looked in the mirror and saw what God sees? That is the superior challenge when we view what God has done for us in Christ. There is no telling what would and could happen.

A Case for True Christianity

What exactly does Christianity really bring to the table? Does it really provide anything of value?

There are a lot of people in the Christian loop (and out) who would passionately answer, "Not a whole heck of a lot." The trend today in those forty and under is to not be that impressed with Christianity. They generally do not sport the same lenses that their parents or grandparents wore. In fact, in many instances, the lenses they don are scratched, broken, and in need of a complete replacement. In fact, young people are not only not that impressed or moved by Christianity but also quite illiterate when it comes to its teachings. Personal experience has trumped biblical truth, and it has produced a church that is a mile high and an inch deep! We truly live in what many call a "post-Christian era." Yet, all is never lost when God is a part of the mix! We can honestly admit that there are indeed a lot of problems with Christendom in its current form. Yet, consider this thought:

If the founder of Christianity, Jesus Christ, is perfect and totally together (and I believe He is), then Christianity must be perfect and totally together in its substance as well!

Chew on that for a bit. In other words, the war-torn "Christian" message must be sufficient for the world's ills, or you can bet that Jesus would have introduced something better! But I think I have an idea on one of the reasons why people are so disillusioned with Christianity and its bold approach. I have thought about this for a few decades, and here's my take (for what it's worth):

Christianity to most people—and even to most Christians—is what I call "an add-on" religion rather than a way of life. It has become a faith that is characterized by the things that you do rather than a vibrant, living faith that focuses on the character of what you become because of the faith that you hold.

Read it again because it is a long sentence, but one in which I have carefully crafted every word.

Biblical Christianity spelled out in the Newer Testament is far more than just a creed or something we do or belong to. *So . . .* what do I mean when I say Christianity has become an "add-on" faith, and how does that relate to understanding eternal salvation?

Christianity as a *Creed* Rather than a Relationship

Somehow, we have come to believe in our churches that the Christian life has more to do with how we *act* than who we are and what our personal relationship toward Christ actually is. We have allowed the enemy to minimize a simplistic walk with Christ (2 Cor. 11:3) to a frenzy of activity that somehow "proves" our spirituality and devotion to Christ. Yet, if religious activity and work were meant to prove our "spiritual temperature," then a growing, transparent, resting relationship with our Savior is, in fact, needless and pointless. Think about it. That is actually what Paul is saying in Galatians 2:21:

"I do not nullify the grace of God, for if righteousness were through the law, then Christ died for no purpose" (ESV).

Christ died needlessly if our works and righteousness are good enough to pull salvation and the Christian life off! The Christian life is not only difficult to live; it is more than that. It is impossible to live apart from the grace of God and the working of His Spirit in us (Gal. 5:16–25). But it goes even deeper than that. We have come to believe that Christianity is a set of beliefs to adhere to rather than a real relationship with a real Savior to enjoy. Creed has in essence replaced communion. What God wants to do through us has been subtly replaced by what we must do for God. We are so hung up on the "laws" of the Christian faith that we are missing the Lawgiver badly. Let me say it this way. We are seeking the "blessing" all the while bypassing the "Blesser" . . . who is blessed forever!

Listen, the Christian faith to many outside of the faith can be reduced to a set of codes, beliefs, and commands that they could never keep in a million years. So they reason, "Why try?" They are convinced that Christianity is too hard to have as their lifestyle, and they believe that Christ rules too much with an "iron fist." If all you believe about the Christian faith is that you are unable to carry it out, then you will be defeated before you leave your bedroom. If you are weighed down by the expectations you think God has for you in your daily life, you will undoubtedly be shut down before you begin. If you are bent on keeping the commands of God with all your fleshly might daily, then you will miss the *relationship* part of Christianity, which by the way, is why Jesus Christ came!

Revelation 3:20 is a beautiful verse. Though it is often used as a verse that supports the need for people to receive Christ, it is really not primarily that when you view its context.

First, it was written to a real church. It was not a mass text to the multitudes.

Second, it is clear that Christ is speaking to His own children because of the verses that precede verse 20 and the content of the verses that follow. The main point of Revelation 3:20 is about intimate fellowship with Christ that comes naturally out of a vibrant *relationship* with Christ. Yet, in this church, Christ was *outside* the door, not inside it. The impact of this cannot be understated.

When Jesus Christ reached you and me in our "sin stupor" and made us a new creation, He did so in order that we could enjoy a real, vital relationship with Him, moment by moment. We will talk later in this book about how we live this Christian life successfully, but for now, we must understand that Christianity is more than a creed or a set of beliefs. It is certainly that, but if it is not *more* than that or *mainly* that, then we have lost the most thrilling piece of the gospel message, which is relationship over rules! I heard it said many years ago that "rules without relationship lead to rebellion." Yes, it does. In a family. In a nation. In a church. In a life. And that is where we are in the church. Quiet rebellion reigns. Christians doing their best to hold one foot firm in the "Christ-less culture" and one in the land of Christ. That, my friend, does not remotely work! Jesus said plainly that we could not "two-time" Him and have it work out. The truth is, that deceptive concept misses out on the essence of the Christian faith—mainly, our love relationship with Jesus. Without this love relationship, we are just punching the time clock in our churches and going through the motions in the religious circles we run in, and we were "re-created" in Christ for much more than that!

Christianity as a Good "Crutch"

If you have ever hurt your leg or ankle, you may have had to use crutches for an extended period of time. Crutches to me were a royal pain. They were awkward and they bothered my underarms, to boot. Yet, I had to admit that they were certainly necessary to me in the healing process. They allowed me the time I needed for my injury to begin to get better; and without them, the healing time, and really, the opportunity for healing—would have changed dramatically.

By its very nature, Christianity is a healing religion. Some would argue that Christianity does the very opposite—conquer and divide. Not *true* Christianity! Not the religion that was first called the Way by those who knew about its Founder—the *Way*! Not the way of life founded by the perfect and completely loving Jesus Christ. Anything or anyone that offers less than healing when presenting Christianity is a cheap, shabby imitation, and imitations have no place in the classic and true gospel of God. Agreed? Let's continue.

Christianity, when it is lived out properly and gracefully, is a wonderful "crutch" to lean on. This world is filled with disappointment, heartache, and pain. Why not "lean" on God for all that you face or will face. To know Him is to trust Him—and to trust Him is the best life of all. But there is certainly another side to Christianity, so let's boldly talk about it.

Christianity as a Bad "Crutch"

The form or the notion of Christianity has been undeniably used for evil in this world. That is certainly inexcusable and lame. Most would point to the Crusades of old or the blowing up of abortion clinics "in the name of God" or the downright hatred of homosexuals as proof that Christians are a "dangerous bunch." And their arguments are not totally off base. But while those events have clearly given Christianity a major black eye, I believe that there is something *else* even more destructive going on.

It is the simple cheapening of the pure Christian message by the slipshod way so-called Christians live.

I have often wondered why God choose to give the most important, eternal message in the universe to flawed, sinful human beings. We seem to mess it up more than we should. God would have certainly been right if He would have taken the job alone, but He hasn't.

A number of years ago, I read a book by Steve Arterburn entitled *Toxic Faith: Experiencing Healing from Painful Spiritual Abuse.* In his book, Arterburn, among other things, underscored the reality of Christians who are long on words and short on love, honesty, and truth. Theirs is what he called a "toxic faith." They are models of Christianity being the "worst" crutch of all because they use their faith for license to live however and wherever their dysfunction will take them. Arterburn in essence confirms that the lack of healing by Christ in their lives is evident by the instability they exude in their own personal life and witness. That is an example of using Christianity as a shameful crutch, and it is both nauseating to God, and of course, to others.

Christianity's Real Intention

So we need to ask and answer in detail these questions: What was and is Christianity's intention or goal? What is it intended to do in the lives of those who embrace its message? The message of true, biblical Christianity is a message that cannot be compared to any other religion in the world. The apostle Paul said this plainly when he wrote, "Christ is the end of the law to everyone who believes"(Rom. 10:4, ESV). That is, when you find Christ, He is the last stop on life's track. You stop striving and searching for the truth and meaning of life. *He* is what you are looking for, though at the time of your salvation, you have no way of understanding that fully.

The great Bible commentator Matthew Henry reminds us, "Those who teach by their doctrine must teach by their life, or else they pull down with one hand what they build up with the other."[19]

The apostle Paul reminded the Ephesian believers in chapter 4, verse 1: "I therefore, a prisoner for the Lord, urge you to walk in a manner worthy of the calling to which you have been called" (ESV). This same apostle reminds his young son in the faith Timothy of this: "For God saved us and **called** us to live a holy life. He did this, not because we deserved it, but because that was his plan from before the beginning of time—to show us his grace through Christ Jesus" (2 Tim. 1:9, NLT; emphasis mine).

As we said earlier, Bible character and religious duty go hand in hand. You cannot have one without

---

[19] Matthew Henry, *The Matthew Henry Study Bible—KJV*, (Peabody, MA: Hendrickson, 2010), 2054.

the other and hope to have spiritual balance and divine success in your life. You may have never thought about that, but it is high time you hear it. We need to discover (maybe *rediscover*) together how we go about living our Christian life from the calling that all of us have received as children of God.

When I was seventeen years old, I truly believed God called me to serve Him in "the marketplace." I was planning on going to Temple University in Philadelphia, Pennsylvania, to pursue a degree in radio and television broadcasting. I was truly excited with the prospects of that, but in the span of twelve months, everything changed. In the interim, I gave Christ the reins of my life, and not long after, through a series of "God events," a clear confirmation catapulted me into a mindset of preparing for full-time Christian ministry. I have never looked back. Now, as great and as amazing that the call to the ministry is—and as thankful I was and am that God counted me faithful, placing me in pastoral ministry—that calling seems small and immaterial when compared to the calling I want to talk about for the next few pages.

God's Divine Call for All of Us, His Children

How would you define "a call from God"?

Romans 11:29 reminds us that "God's gifts and his **call** can never be withdrawn" (NLT; emphasis mine).

So what does that mean, exactly? Let me share a few more verses on God's calling of you and me and how that plays in to the identity driven life.

1 Corinthians 1:26 (NIV): "Brothers and sisters, think of what you were when you were **called**

[emphasis mine]. Not many of you were wise by human standards; not many were influential; not many were of noble birth."

Ephesians 1:18 (NLT): "I pray that your hearts will be flooded with light so that you can understand the confident hope he has given to those he **called** [emphasis mine]—his holy people who are his rich and glorious inheritance."

2 Thessalonians 1:11 (ESV): "To this end we always pray for you, that our God may make you worthy of his **calling** [emphasis mine] and may fulfill every resolve for good and every work of faith by his power. . . ."

2 Timothy 1:9 (NIV): "He has saved us and **called** [emphasis mine] us to a holy life—not because of anything we have done but because of his own purpose and grace. This grace was given us in Christ Jesus before the beginning of time. . . ."

The words "chose" and "call" are often used interchangeably in the Scriptures. In other words, whom God calls, He chooses. So the question is, what about this calling or choosing? What is it and why do I need to know and love its truth as a child of God?

First, whom God chooses or calls, He calls forever.

That's what Romans 11:29 says—the **calling** [of God; emphasis mine] cannot be withdrawn. God calls people to Himself as lost souls, but once they are recipients of His love calling, they are "found" souls and His forever. That is what Bible teachers commonly call "eternal security."

Eternal security is a biblical teaching that says that once you are truly saved by God's grace, you will always and forever be saved. Now, I admit that there

are enough good, Christ-loving Christians who do
not believe that salvation is forever under any and/
or all circumstances. But I do, and I simply believe it
principally because of the nature of God's salvation.
Let me illustrate for a moment what I mean.

I am the son of Albert Gregas. I know that I
could disown my father by going to court and legally
forfeiting his fatherhood over me. I know that I could
at any time choose to cut him out of my life and ignore
him. I know that I could displease him to the point
where he might cut me off in some way. But there is
one big problem that remains: I have Al Gregas's DNA
and blood coursing through my veins. I am (at least,
in this life) one with him as he is one with me. Today,
and as long as I live, I cannot deny that nor can I do
anything to disrupt or nullify this natural truth.

In the same way, we are spiritually planted into
Christ, and we are one with Him as much as He is
with us. We are intimately joined to Him, and His
eternal DNA is running through our spiritual veins so
that we are "eternally secure" in His Son. We cannot
do anything to disrupt or nullify this truth. Why?
Because it is how God wired it. That is the ultimate
gift of God's calling. We become His glad and precious
property forever. Praise His Name!

Second, God wants us to live in accordance with
our calling.

That is exactly what Paul is after when he
transitions his thoughts in Ephesians chapter 4, verse
1. If you read the first three chapters of Ephesians,
you will notice that the apostle does not ask one thing
of the Ephesians relative to their walk with God. In
chapters 1 through 3, the Holy Spirit centers in on

the life and position of the believer in Christ and what all that means. But there is a clear line drawn between chapters 3 and 4. In chapter 4, verse 1, Paul transitions and effectively marries character and duty rather beautifully. Notice his words:

Therefore I, a prisoner for serving the Lord, beg you to lead a life worthy of your calling, for you have been called by God (NLT).

What is Paul getting at, exactly? This: God wants us to live in accordance with our calling. He might say it like this. Are you a believer in Jesus Christ by *position*? Your answer: Yes. Then be a believer in Jesus Christ by *condition*. Are you a believer by the *work of Christ* applied to your life? Your answer: Yes. Then be a believer in your *walk for Christ* in life. That is: *Live like you are*. If you're the president, then live like you are; don't live like you are like everyone else. If you are rich, then do not imitate the lives of those in dire poverty. If you are holy in Christ, then walk in a life of holiness. Why? Because that is who you are—that's why!

Our walk should match our talk, right? Not perfectly, but persistently. No one should be able to look at our way of life and be able to honestly say, "If that is what a Christian is, I want no part of it!" In all we think, say, and do, we should walk worthy as children of God. We should walk worthy of the vocation, the calling, to which we have been called. That is the supernatural response to being called by God, and it is the clarion call of every true follower of the Master.

Finally, this calling from God in Christ is a heavenly calling.

Hebrews 3:1 tells us, "Therefore, holy brothers, you who share in a heavenly calling, consider Jesus, the apostle and high priest of our confession . . ." (ESV).

Our calling from God is not an earthly, culturally based calling. It is one that is stamped with the mark of Heaven itself. We can no longer be apathetic about our place in God's family. Our calling is on purpose by the will of God. Do not think that your salvation is just something that was "in the cards." It is specifically part of the sovereign plan of God before the galaxies were hung. Don't ever forget that. Heaven engineered it and heaven carries it out (Phil. 1:6).

Part II

Five Principles about Spiritual Identity That Every Christian Must Know and Understand

Identity Truth #1

You Are Who God Says You Are (Part 2)

6

Suffering from Spiritual Identity Theft

"You didn't even know you got your pocket picked, did you? Spiritual identity theft is on the rise, and too often we don't even know it's happening. In fact, most people live in a constant state of crisis: spiritual identity crisis. How can we feel so close to God one moment and totally turn our backs on Him the next? How can we have days of incredible spiritual victories followed by periods of intense defeat? And . . . how can you recover the rest of you?"[20]

Satan wants you to be somebody you're not and he wants you to become someone you were never meant to be.

Financial identity theft is huge and extremely debilitating. I am sure that some, maybe many, who

---

[20] "Identity Theft," Elevation Church, sermon series by Pastor Steven Furtick, http://elevationchurch.org/sermons/identitytheft.

are reading this chapter can relate to identity theft. It is annoying in every way. Yet, there is a far more damaging "identity theft" going on in the world, and specifically, in the lives of God's children. Just for the record, I am aware that the culture of the unbelieving has its own issues as it relates to spiritual identity theft. We will explore that in some detail, as well, in the pages that follow. Yet, this theft of identity that has infiltrated the body of Christ like a lethal disease is both shameful and sure. It must be talked about and acknowledged. God's people do not know who they are, and the sad thing is, many "do not know what they do not know." Something has to change, and something must be discovered. That's for sure.

That is our goal in this chapter—to clearly explain how most of us reading this book are suffering badly from spiritual identity theft and that we probably are not even aware of it. I can hear a few of you saying. "So what, Chris. How does that make any major difference in my life?" You will not be asking that in a few minutes. I promise you that.

Eric Geiger, in his very insightful book *Identity*, relates a story that demonstrates how far identity theft can go. He writes about a man named Brian Jackson who wanted to be a Pittsburgh Steeler like nobody's business. So he did what few of us would do. He turned his dream into a reality. The only problem was—it was of his own deceptive doing. He became, in his own mind, what he was not. Brian studied the players he wanted to "become," and when he was done, he lived out their lives. His obsession for "being" the player allowed him to fool a lot of people for a long time. To one girl, he was Jerame Tuman, the Steelers' tight end. To another girl, he was Big Ben Roethlisberger. To still another, he was Brian St. Pierre. He signed footballs, recounted stories, and in essence, "became" these players to unsuspecting fans.[21] He was, as they say, "living the dream" until the dream turned ugly.

Brian got busted—shown to be a fanatical fake. Those who had believed him discovered through pictures and TV spots that this guy was not who he said he was. Brian faced felony charges for identity theft. It is telling to hear what he says about the whole thing: "I just idolized these guys and what they do, and the attention they get from women, and I just want that for myself, and I don't think I can do that on my own, and I just want to be them."[22] How true and sad it is that we will go to such lengths to be noticed and valued. It is true that to be loved and appreciated is innate in all of us. How we get there is another matter. We should not think for a moment that this guy is in a league all his own. If we are honest (yes, that includes me!), all of us play out a similar part out in our lives daily with the hope of filling that gigantic hole in the depth of our soul. Probably not to this extreme; but nonetheless, we play a similar game.

Today, let's discover what we are missing when it comes to spiritual identity. If we are going to be all that Christ intended, it simply cannot be attained without coming to grips with our true identity. We must see what is happening behind the scenes, robbing us from all that Christ has for us.

---

[21] Eric Geiger, *Identity* (Nashville: B&H Publishing Group, 2008), n.p.
[22] Justin Heckert, "I'm with the Steelers," *ESPN The Magazine*, May 7, 2007, 103.

Identity Theft's Familiar Road

As I stated, I am more convinced today than ever before: Satan wants you to be somebody you're not and he wants you to become someone you were never meant to be.

How does he accomplish this? Through spiritual identity theft.

What does identity theft in the spiritual realm mean?

Satan's goal is to keep us from enjoying the privileges we have in Christ. And he, for the last two thousand years, has unfortunately scored very high marks in this regard. Before we get into "redeeming" our identity and taking back what the Devil has stolen from us, we need to talk a bit more about the "characteristics" of financial identity theft so we can get a clearer picture.

What are the chief characteristics of identity theft?

Characteristic #1: Identity theft is the fastest growing crime in the Western world.

I would also say that, particularly in the West, spiritual identity theft seems to be more prevalent as well. The striking parallels in the natural and spiritual world center around what J. I. Packer refers to as a "hot-tub" mentality that permeates our two cultures. We are too relaxed, often lazy and irresponsible, and identity theft multiplies and festers in such an environment.

Characteristic #2: It takes an average victim an estimated $500 and thirty hours to resolve each identity theft crime.

If that is true with financial identity theft, then how much time is lost, and how much of our spiritual resources are squandered, by wandering through life not knowing what our true identity actually is? There is no way to measure how much we miss in the work of Christ by not living out our identity in Christ!

Characteristic #3: Studies have shown that those closest to us (friends, family, neighbors, and fellow employees) are the ones who steal our identity.

That was a shocker to me when I first read that. But then I thought, though in the spiritual realm we wrestle not against flesh and blood, but against satanic powers, we often allow people close to us to define who we are. In essence, they are given permission to "steal our identities," making us ineffective for the kingdom of God. Often it is hard to admit that those who are closest to us are the ones who greatly assist in dragging us down, making us useless in our stand for Christ. It's not their fault, but they are often ready to lead us onto dysfunctional island.

Characteristic #4: Most cases of identity theft can be resolved if they are caught early enough.

That is hopeful. So it is in the spiritual world. The earlier you can biblically define your identity, the better off you will be in the service of Christ. The damage, of course, is much more lethal as the years multiply. So what are we to do if we believe that we have been the victim of spiritual identity theft? I'm glad you asked.

Let's discuss how you and I can be successfully restored from the ill effects of spiritual identity theft.

Who You Are from God's Point of View

Let me define how we perceive our identity again so we're on the same page. It is the way we see ourselves. The way we value ourselves. The way we determine whether we are loved or worth something to someone. The challenge of getting spiritual identity right is seeing ourselves correctly, no matter how we feel, what we believe, or even what others say about us.

In the spiritual realm, it is who you really *are*, not who others think you are or even who you think you are. We've got to be convinced that what God thinks is really the chief thing that matters when all is said and done! He is the final voice on the matter. If you question that, do you have anyone else that would be qualified to make this determination? If God is the most powerful person in the universe and He knows all things, don't you think what He says should be strongly considered and adopted quickly?

What God thinks of us as Christians is what the New Testament describes as our "identity in Christ." That is why knowing our true spiritual identity affects our behavior, our attitudes, our values, our feelings—everything that we are is affected by what we think of ourselves.

Cultural Ways of Defining Our Value and Worth

Let me remind you of how the culture (and, I am afraid, far too many "churchians") measures their worth, value, and acceptance. We are talking here about the tape measure, or the mechanism, for how our culture values our value. These ways are, in fact, what the world lives by and is unfortunately enslaved to. And—these ways fall way, way short of realistically measuring true value and worth. Here goes.

1. Our possessions or the things we have. You've heard the mantra: "He who has the most toys in life at the end of life—wins!"

There are so many people who believe that. There is a big problem with that philosophy. Jesus said in essence that a person's life does *not* bring value or worth through the abundance of things that he possesses . . . (Luke 12:15). Finding our value and worth from what we own, have, or may accumulate is not only foolish and empty but also is not God's path to true fulfillment and personal security. So we have to close the door on this method, because it doesn't work.

2. Our appearance and outward looks. That is, what we look like on the outside with the aid of clothes, a certain hairstyle, a tan or no tan, what our face looks like, body type etc. . . .

There is a big problem with believing this. The Scriptures say that God does not look at our **outward appearance**, he looks at our heart (1 Sam. 16:7; emphasis mine). Not only that, but the Bible says, "Charm is deceiving and outward appearance is fleeting and a bubble that will soon burst" (Prov. 31:30). Many people value themselves by what they look like or what they think they look like. But have you ever been to a funeral and looked at someone lying in the casket? Do you really believe that what you see is all there is to that person—at that moment? Finding our value and worth from what we look like or believe we look like is not only unwise and empty but also is not God's path to fulfillment and personal security. Besides, if there was a certain "look" that made us valuable and worthy–don't you think God would have made us all the same with that look? Just sayin'! So, again, we have to close the door on this popular method. It doesn't work.

3. Knowledge and education. This is what we know and learn in life through the study of certain subjects or disciplines.

Is there anything *wrong* with being knowledgeable and educated? Not at all. The prophet Hosea quotes God when he says my people are dying and wasting away because of their lack of knowledge (Hosea 4:6). God certainly does not put a premium on stupidity, but does he overly celebrate and favor (like our culture does) those who are highly educated and refined? Not at all.

What is the big problem with getting our worth, value, and security from our intellectual knowledge and broad education? Well, for starters, the Scriptures state, "The knowledge of the world is **foolishness** with God . . . (1 Cor. 1:27; emphasis mine). In Jeremiah 9, the prophet Jeremiah warns us in verse 23 that we should **not** boast in our knowledge and learning. It is, in the end, a bubble that bursts! If God measured our value and worth based on our brain power, He would have made all of us with the same brain power. Right? It would be grossly unfair to many of us in this world if God measured value and worth based on our intelligence or our diligence in academia. I am so glad that He doesn't do that. So we have to close the door on this method as well. It simply doesn't work.

4. Our popularity or people groups that we belong to. This is who we are because of whom we know, or being a part of the "in crowd." Our belief that popularity and notoriety equals personal worth.

Yet, this begs the question, popular in whose eyes? *God's?* There is only one popular and famous person in God's address book and it is—His beloved Son, in whom He is completely pleased! What is the enduring problem with finding our value and worth in whom we know or in who knows and recognizes us?

The *Scriptures* say that God does not play favorites or politics (James 2:1-10), and He is not impressed with whom we know or who we think we are! Our call as His children is "to play to the audience of One"— namely, Jesus Christ. Anything less is to become what the apostle Paul calls a "people pleaser" rather than a God pleaser. The apostle warned his young son in the faith, Timothy, that in the last days before Jesus returns, the world culture would be characterized by this egocentric kind of thinking and living, so we should not be surprised by its hold on society. Popular to whom? Certain people? A specific group? So what? What is that ultimately paying out?

Have you not learned that these same people can turn on you in a New York minute? Then where's your value and worth? It's in the toilet, isn't it? God's design is never for His people to live by what others think of them, good or bad. So we have to close the door on this method. It simply doesn't work.

5. How people treat or have treated us. Let me ask you an important question: Are you going to let someone or a group of people tell you how valuable you are, how much worth you have, and how loved you really are by how they treat you? Really? Why would you do that? Did they make you? Do they really care the most about you in this world? Do they perfectly have your best interest in mind? *Really?* Finding our value and worth from how people view us or treat us is not only unwise and empty but also can never lead us to God's way of peace and joy. If this is a dead end (and it absolutely is), then why waste your time any longer on this nonsense?

If we find our value in what others think of us or how they have treated us or abused us or rejected us, then most, if not all, of us have little chance of enjoying a hopeful, confident, peaceful Christian life—the life which Christ died to give us! This method doesn't work either.

6. Religious affiliation or group we worship with. This is our religious and spiritual position in our place of worship and in this world. This is a real popular one, and it is difficult to convince people of this "false measurement"! What is the real problem with finding our worth, value, and a sense of belonging in "religion or the church"?

Well, first, religion is manmade. All of the religious systems of the world, without exception, are founded on the false idea that man has the ability within himself to reach out and/or up to God by his own works and supposed goodness! There is one slight (really, major) problem with that kind of thinking. The Bible is dead set against that belief, and it also steals God of His own glory and grace.

Someone said, "Some people have just enough religion to make themselves miserable." Isn't that the truth? If religion could give us the value and love we long for, then Jesus would have never visited Earth and suffered an awesomely painful death for us. Religion doesn't need Jesus. It never has. Religions around the world may pay reverence to Jesus in some way, but they are, in the end, convinced that their religious affiliation or passion is the ticket to paradise. So we have to close the door on this method as well. It simply doesn't work.

7. Our good works and deeds which, we reason, equal our personal righteousness. How many of you, before you came to Christ, believed that your good deeds counted for something in God's eyes? That they gave you a fair amount of value and worth in God and man's eyes? If you did, let me share a big problem with that kind of thinking.

The big problem is the Scriptures clearly say, "Not by works of righteousness that we have done, but by *His mercy He saved us*" (Titus 3:5; italics mine), and "by [God's] grace (unmerited favor) are we saved through faith and that not of yourselves, it is a gift of God, not as a results of good works, that no one should be able to boast (Eph. 2: 9). We must remember that our good works before we know Christ and even after we know Christ do not give us value and worth! Isaiah, the prophet, said that all our righteousness is like filthy rags (Isa. 64:6). That pretty much sums up what our righteousness looks like through the lenses of a perfect God. Filthy, rotten, stinky rags!

Now all these "false measurements" concerning what is important and valued in our world is, according to Jesus, "an abomination to the Lord" (Luke 16:15). That's pretty strong language. An abomination by its very root means "to disgust." So that means trusting in the wrong measurements of value and importance is literally "disgusting" to God, and it should be to us. Besides, these false measurements simply don't work effectively or eternally, so why would we ever employ them into our daily life? It is truly a waste of time!

So . . . if our true value—how we feel about ourselves, our worth, and our love—does not come from possessions, appearance, education, popularity, how others treat us, religious affiliation, or our good deeds and righteousness, then where does it come from?

Here's the bottom line: Our true identity must come from another source other than ourselves or others! It must come from other than what life and the culture can offer us. Does that make sense to you? Are you with me? So, where do we go from here? What is our next move?

Here are our choices.

Are we going to trust people who personally don't have all the answers for their own lives, let alone ours? Are we going to let others tell us who we are and why we are valuable or worth something? Are we going to believe the "lies" that we have been told or believe the feelings that we have, which by the way, cannot be fully and reliably trusted? Are we going to live to be somebody special by what we do or by what others say about us?

Or . . .

Are we going to believe what God says about us? Who is "this God" we are talking to according to the Bible? He is

- Totally perfect in person and character
- Totally all-knowing in every way
- Unconditionally loving towards His creation
- The One who cares most about you because He made you and invested in you at the cross
- Not going to fail you or bail on you
- Not going to ever lie to you, but will always shoot straight with you.

Now if you don't believe in that kind of God, you will never be spiritually free! You also will never enjoy the assurance and security of the identity driven life! I want you to know, as for me, I am going with the second choice.

Why? Simply because God has the final word on us His creation. And His news is great news for all of those who are family. This hope is for every adult, teen, and child, no matter who they might be. If we are willing to believe and receive this God verdict, it has the potential to change the direction and motivation of our Christian life forever. That sounds to me like we better not pass on that offer! Let's build on this in the upcoming chapter.

7

You Are Who God Says You Are

Who in God's Name Are You?

"Nothing is more foundational to your freedom from Satan's bondage than understanding and affirming what God has done for you in Christ and who you are as a result. We all live in accordance with our perceived identity."

–Dr. Neil Anderson

Who you are (or think you are) is the most important thing about you.

A well-known speaker started off his seminar by holding up a $100 bill. In the room of two hundred, he asked, "Who would like this $100 bill?" Hands started going up. He said, "I am going to give this $100 bill to one of you; but first, let me do this." He proceeded to crumple the $100 dollar bill up. He then asked, "Who still wants it?" Still, the hands were up in the air. "Well," he continued, "what if I do this?" And he dropped it on the ground and started to grind it into the floor with his shoe. He picked the bill up, now crumpled and dirty. "Now, who still wants it?" Still, the hands went into the air. "My friends," the speaker said, "we have all learned a very valuable lesson. No matter what I did to the money, you still wanted it because it did not decrease in value. It was still worth $100."

Many times in our lives, we are dropped, crumpled, and ground into the dirt by the decisions others have made and the decisions we have made. We feel as though we are worthless and unusable. But no matter what has happened or what will happen, you will never lose your value. Dirty or clean, crumpled or finely creased, you are still priceless to the One who loves you most.

Let's talk about that in this chapter.

If you were to ask you who you are, how would you respond? You might give me your name, and I would say that is just your name. Or, I am a sales person and I would say, no—that is what you do. Again, I ask you, who are you, and you say I am a Christian, and once more, the answer shouts back loud and clear: no, that is your Christian stripe, but that is not the real you. I hope by now you are getting the point. The question of who we are is not an easy one to answer, is it? If it were, then there would be no reason for this book, let alone this chapter. Most of us have come to believe that the essence of "us" is connected to what we *are* in life, what we *do* in life, and even how others *perceive* us to be. That is just the natural stream of thinking, and because our culture beats this into us rather successfully for years on end, it is hard to think and believe any other way.

In his book *Rough Road to Freedom,* Dr. Neil Anderson writes, "Why don't we know who we are? That question dogged me for years. Is this a conscious awareness that we grow into, and therefore part of the growth process? That seemed to fit my experience. Or did God intend this truth to be the foundation from which we grow? If you search Scripture, which I did, you have to come to the conclusion that our identity and position in Christ is *foundational* [italics mine]. The apostle Paul taught that we need to be firmly rooted in Christ in order to grow in Christ, and see to it that we are not carried away by human traditions and elementary principles of the world" (Col. 2:6–10).[23]

That is at the root of what I want to talk about in this chapter. I truly have come to believe that who we are is the most important thing about us. Solomon, the wisest mortal who ever lived (the Bible makes that claim; that is not my opinion), said it this way, "As a man thinks in his heart, so he becomes." (Prov. 23:7, KJV) In other words, what we believe dictates what we do. Put another way, our beliefs motivate our actions. So it would do us real well to believe the right things about ourselves, because what we believe about ourselves will certainly lead us to live a predetermined way. Hopefully "that way" is for the glory and pleasure of Christ (2 Cor. 5:9–10). That is God's goal for us in Christ.

One of the great passages in the Newer Testament that pounds home the whole identity-before-purpose theme is found in 1 Peter 2:9–12. We have already said that Paul primarily was chosen by God to herald this

---

[23] Neil T. Anderson, *Rough Road to Freedom* (Oxford, England: Monarch Books-Lion Hudson, 2012), 129.

divine order, but Peter, in his first letter, also allows the Holy Spirit to paint this order beautifully. Notice his words: position first and condition second.

> But you are a chosen race, a royal priesthood, a holy nation, a people for his own possession, that you may proclaim the excellencies of him who called you out of darkness into his marvelous light. Once you were not a people, but now you are God's people; once you had not received mercy, but now you have received mercy. Beloved, I urge you as sojourners and exiles to abstain from the passions of the flesh, which wage war against your soul. Keep your conduct among the Gentiles honorable, so that when they speak against you as evildoers, they may see your good deeds and glorify God on the day of visitation. (ESV)

Peter, in the first two chapters of this letter, lays down what God in Christ has done for each believer. In verses 9 and 10 of chapter 2, Peter takes the time to encourage the believers that were scattered, saying, here is what you are ("you are a chosen race, a royal priesthood, a holy nation, a people for his own possession . . ." so that [for the purpose of] "you may proclaim the excellencies of him who called you out of darkness into his marvelous light . . ."), knowing who we are in God's eyes can allow us to "be" a witness (notice not "do witnessing") of what He has done in our lives. Peter goes on to say that we were "once not God's people but now we are," not because of what we have done but because we are a glad heir of His mercy. What is mercy? Not getting what we deserve, which, according to the Scriptures is–*death* (Rom. 6:23; italics mine).

Not until Peter lays the identity groundwork does he then say that we are to live out what we have, in fact, been "called" to. Verse 11 starts a list of commands and responsibilities that he wants his readers to take seriously and soberly.

> Beloved, I urge you as sojourners and exiles to abstain from the passions of the flesh, which wage war against your soul. Keep your conduct among the Gentiles honorable, so that when they speak against you as evildoers, they may see your good deeds and glorify God on the day of visitation.

Even in verse 11, Peter calls the believers "sojourners and exiles," and that is certainly who we are as a child of God. (Still another identity trait as a child of God.) Knowing who you are, Peter says, motivates us to abstain from fleshly advances, live honorably among men, and allow our works to bring great glory to God (verse 11–12, summarized). Let me ask you a question:

Do you think it is important to know what God thinks about you if you are going to be confident and successful in serving Him? Would you be rightly energized and empowered by someone who constantly barked out orders to you? If you knew they were unhappy with you and they didn't really like you or support you?

The answer is, of course not! Unfortunately, that is how it is with so many of God's people. They have grown up believing (or have come to believe) that God is really not for them, but rather is more interested in them getting their act together . . . the sooner the better. Their Christian experience is summed up in the deep feeling of never being good enough for God to use them or bless them. I have seen this over and over again, and it is a sham and a scandal across the Christian landscape.

(Very important disclaimer: You must be a child of God to enjoy the truth of your spiritual identity. If you are not, then these truths CAN be yours to claim, but not in your present spiritual state.)

Do you want to feel better about yourself? Do you want to believe you are loved for who you are and for not what you do? Do you want to know that you are accepted no matter who you are? Do you want to know that you are worth something to someone other than another human being? You can if you would only believe and receive what God says about you!!

Remember: these truths have nothing to do what you feel, what others have said about you, or even what you believe about yourself.

So what does He say about you and me?

Identity Truth #1: You are who God says you are.

If we are ever going to be all that God desires; if we are ever going to be at peace with ourselves and God; if we are ever going to get past the deep ruts and healing from the scarring incisions of our past, we are going to have to believe what God says about us. Why shouldn't we? We have believed for a lifetime the lies the Devil has been dealing out. Many of us have mistakenly built our lives on shifting, undependable sand rooted in a core belief that says our worth and value is in "us." That we must become the best version of ourselves. That in "us" and our strength, we have the power to become all that God intended. Those lies have made us look good on the outside (at least, some of us) but have kept us usefully reckless and broken in our spiritual influence. God made us to know Him intimately, and the only way we can do that is to believe Him without reservation.

Who Is It That God Says You Are?

Who is it that God says you are? Let's talk about it. By the way, all of these statements pertaining to who you are, according to God, are found in the word of God, the Bible. They then are completely true and reliable, no matter how you may feel or what you have come to believe about yourself.

Here is what is true of every person that belongs to Christ. Read it and weep!

You are God's child. You belong to the greatest family in the universe, and you are not the "middle or youngest" child in the family. God does not have grandkids, and he doesn't have kids that are closer in position to Him. His inheritance is to *all* his kids, baring none! (John 1:12). Say "I am God's child."

You are Christ's friend. You are friends with the God of the universe. Think about that for a moment. I don't know how many friends you have or what they are like, but "he is a friend that sticks closer than a family member" (John 15:15). Say "I am Christ's friend."

You are in right standing with God. The Bible calls this being "justified." That is, to be declared totally righteous in God's sight. When God looks at you, He sees you wrapped in the perfect robe of His Son, no sin and no past (Rom. 5:1). Say "I am in right standing with God."

You are in partnership with Christ. What better "partner" can you have in the divine business you have been called to than Jesus Himself? You are co-laborers with Him (1 Cor. 6:17). Say "Christ is my divine business partner."

You are God's own, and you belong to Him. God is your owner now, and you are His and He is yours. What a secure relationship you have with Him (1 Cor. 6:20). Say "I am God's and I belong to Him."

You are a member of Christ's body. You are a valued member of His team. There is no team in this world that can compare to being on Christ's team. He is a winner in every season, and so are you (1 Cor. 12:27). Say "I am a member of Christ's body."

You are a saint. You are set apart and uniquely God's. Not being your effort, but solely based on Christ's work on the cross. Sainthood in the world is based on your good life and supernatural tendencies. Sainthood for the child of God is a gift and position that is given at the moment of salvation, and it has nothing to do with merit or lifestyle (Eph. 1:1). Say "I am a saint of God by salvation."

You are adopted into God's family. You are a full-fledged child and family member of God Almighty. Unlike adoption in our society, all of us who are adopted into the family of God be the new birth are "full-fledged" members of the family with all the rights and privileges of every other family member (Eph. 1:5). Say "I have been adopted into God's family."

You are free to approach God at any time. That is a privilege only afforded to God's children. God is available to talk to and approach at any time and every situation (Eph. 2:18). That is huge because it tells us that He is available to us at any time. I have often said, "God works the night shift." The world cannot think through a God who is willing to listen to us every day, all day. Say "I am free to approach God at any time of the day."

You are forgiven of all of your sins. Every sin and mistake that you have ever committed is under and covered by the blood of Christ. All of your past, present, and even future sins have been wiped out by Jesus Christ. You are positionally perfect in God's sight (2 Cor. 5:21; Col. 1:14). Say "I have been forgiven of all of my sins—past, present, and future."

You are free from sin's domination in your life. Sin no longer has a hold on you to master you. The Christian sins because he *wants* to, not because he *has* to (Col. 1:14). Say "I am free from sin's domination in my life."

You are perfectly whole or complete in Christ. That means that when you have Christ, you have everything (Col. 2:10). You are perfectly equipped for every good work. There is nothing more that we need when we find Jesus. The Bible says that Christ is the "end of the law to everyone who believes." Say "I have everything I need in Christ."

You are free from all guilt and condemnation. You no longer have to live in shame and under condemnation. Christ has set you free from living and feeling that way (Rom. 8:1). Say "I am free from all guilt and shame, now and forever."

You are secure in the love Christ has for you. Christ's love for you is always and forever constant and cannot be received or kept by how you live (Rom. 8:35–39). Say "I am totally secure in the love that Christ has for me."

You are confident and sure that what God started in you, He will complete in you. What God started in your life spiritually, He will finish, which means that He will never give up on you, though you may give up on yourself (Phil. 1:6). Say "What God started in me, He will bring to completion.

You are a citizen of heaven (Phil. 3:20). Your real home or place of residence is not your country down here, but the vast, beautiful country of heaven. You are not home yet, so we cannot live like this life is all there is. Say "I am a citizen of heaven, and this earth is not my real home."

You are hidden with Christ in God (Col. 3:3). This verse lets us know that we are safe and secure in Christ and the Father. No demon can harm us, spiritually speaking, without our consent, and our life is solely in the Father's big hands. Say "I am safe and protected in the arms of Christ."

You are free from fear's grip in your life (2 Tim. 1:7). Because you are one with Christ, fear does not have to empower or control your life. If God is with us, for us, and in us, why do we need to worry or fear what man can do to us? Say "I am free from all Satanic fear in my life."

You are the salt and light of the culture you live in (Matt. 5:13–16). You, as a child of God, have a tremendous influence upon the culture in which you live. Salt preserves and flavors, while light exposes and illumines all that it touches. That's who you are if you would just believe it and walk in it daily. Say "I am the salt and light of my culture."

You are a living branch of Christ, the True Vine (John 15:1, 5). Just as a branch cannot draw strength or life unless it is connected to the vine, so we cannot do so without this vital relationship with the True Vine, the Lord Jesus Christ. As long as we trust and lean on Christ, we will produce spiritual fruit for God in increasing measure, and in the process, please Him. That is what a vine does. There is no struggling to make it happen. It happens as the branch lives in and by the Vine who produces living sap that affects everything and everyone around it. Say "I am a branch in the Vine able to produce spiritual fruit for God."

You (yes, *you*) are a personal witness for Jesus Christ (Acts 1:8). God never asks us to do acts of witnessing. He does call us "witnesses." That means that who we are (His witnesses) reflects and communicates who He is, and that responsibility is the greatest of all. Say "I am a personal witness for the King of Kings and Lord of Lords."

You are an ambassador for Christ (2 Cor. 5:20). You are a personal representative of the King of Kings and Lord of Lords. The world makes its appeal through commercials, but God makes His appeal through Christians. You are the only Bible that some people (before salvation) will ever read. Being an ambassador is a huge privilege, indeed. Say "I am a personal representative for the King of heaven and earth."

You are the righteousness of Christ (2 Cor. 5:21). When you came to Christ at salvation, He took your dirty, stinking righteousness and exchanged it for His perfect, pure righteousness. Which means that when God looks at you now, He does not see your sin, but His Son and the work on the cross that has been applied to your heart by the new birth. Say "I am the perfect righteousness of Christ."

You are seated with Christ in the heavens (Eph. 2:6). Spiritually speaking, you are **already** seated at God's right hand with Jesus. This means that you are an over-comer, a victor, and you have the authority of Jesus to live life not "under" the circumstances but "over" them. Say "I am now seated with Christ at the Father's right hand."

You are God's masterpiece (Eph. 2:10). You are worth a great deal to God. You may not feel or believe that you are, but in God's estimation, you are in Christ, and you are valuable and of eternal worth to God. That ought to let you know that the God of the universe doesn't mistake value like we often do. Say "I am God's masterpiece." (Suggestion: Do this in front of a mirror!)

You are given Christ's power to live the Christian life (Phil. 4:13). "Can't" or "cannot" must not be in the vocabulary of the child of God. The truth is, we can do all things (not some) through the power of Christ, who is our strength. That means that all things are possible to him who believes and trusts in Christ, no matter what it is. Say "I can do all things through Christ, who gives me the strength."

You are enslaved to Jesus Christ (Rom. 1:1; 6:18–22). One of the truths that John MacArthur, in his book, *Slave,* points out that what has been lost for a long time in the Christian church is the idea that once we become free from enslavement to sin positionally (that comes at our conversion moment), we become enslaved to Jesus Christ. Slaves to Christ, not simply "servants" of Christ. Paul told the Corinthians they were no longer their own person, but that they had been bought with a price (1 Cor. 6:18–20), evoking the truth that we now slaves are owned by our Eternal Master, Jesus Christ.

The idea that we can be saved today and Jesus is our Savior today and that we can "rededicate" our lives to Christ later as Lord is found NOWHERE in the New Testament. Say it with me! **NOWHERE**! You and I have been bought by God and we belong to Him. We are His bond-slaves, which means that we do what He says, we answer to His complete bidding, and are His forever with no way of breaking or severing that relationship. What a beautiful truth indeed! Say "I am a slave of Jesus, my Redeemer."

You are a stranger in this world you live in (1 Pet. 2:11). We are not of this world. We are just passing through. The Bible uses the word "alien" to explain the child of God. No wonder we don't fit in this godless culture. There is no way to serve God and things. We will love the one and hate the other. If you feel like you don't belong to this world, you're right. Celebrate the fact that you are not of this world. You were not made and remade in Christ to be. Say "This world is not my home, I am only passing through."

(Special note: This is not an exhaustive list, but it is enough of a list to achieve inward change!)

And here's the best part! Every one of these statements is completely true of you because you are a child of God! You can do *nothing* to make them truer of you. You can; however, make these traits more meaningful if you will just believe and receive them! Are you going to tell me that it is easier for you to not feel or believe you are greatly valued and loved by the One who matters *after* going through this "partial" list?

Here's the key: The more you remind yourself of *who you are in Christ* (who you are), the more your *behavior* (what you do) will begin to mirror your true identity. Did you hear that? Read that sentence again, please.

Knowing these biblical truths provide you the power and the wisdom to live out the Christian life successfully. Someone might be tempted to say at this point, so what? What does knowing these truths do for me or provide me with in this crazy, tough, sin-drenched culture?

Let me give you some application points about this new life as we close this chapter.

First, knowing and receiving these truths allows us to rest in Christ and to not have to strive like the culture for love, acceptance, and a feeling of value.

What happens? Things and experiences and losses do not have a hold on us like they might have or used to. *Why?* Because we now have a strong spiritual foundation that is sure and true.

Second, knowing and receiving these truths best prepares us for life's tragedies and the hard circumstances that come our way.

What happens? Adverse circumstances and life's disappointments only reach the *outer* man rather than destroy the *inner* man. Why? Because we have a strong spiritual foundation now that is sure and true. Adversity can only make you bitter or better. If you don't know who you are in Christ and your mind is not firm in this incredible spiritual union you enjoy with Him, you will not fare well when the great storms of life get up in your grill.

Third, knowing and receiving these truths motivates us to seek God's pleasure more than His approval.

What happens then? We do not live our Christian lives trying to gain an approval from God that has already been given in Christ. Once we grasp and begin to live out our identity in Christ, our works can now flow from a confident assurance in that identity. We no longer have to believe that our spiritual identity is derived from all the good works that we perform. We "be" to "do," not the other way around. Our goal can now be what the great apostle Paul's was in 2 Corinthians 5:9—**to please God**.

The day must come to end when we as God's children believe that the more we do, the more God's pleasure is extended to us. His pleasure is tied to us responding in love to His love. His pleasure is tied to us obeying Him, because to not do so would sadden His heart. Pleasing Him is an overflow of loving Him, and loving Him is a result of no longer living under the law (which kills), but under grace (which gives life—see Romans 6:14–23).

Finally, knowing and receiving these identity truths allow us to be an "exporter" of the freedom we have found in Christ.

Make no mistake. God knows (and so does the Devil) that what you don't *own*, you can't *sell*! Put another way, if you don't have the real goods, you can't share them with anyone!! God has freed us so that we can take the freedom that we have found and spread the wealth! Jesus said it this way: "Freely you have received; freely give." Free people bring freedom to enslaved people. Hurting people just hurt other people. *Which one will you allow God to make you?* It will make all the difference in the world for you and countless others, I can assure you! If you are hurting people regularly, you just prove to be a prime candidate for the grace and freedom God offers in His Son. It's all good.

This passion for knowing who I am in Christ, and in turn sharing it with all who would listen, was really birthed during my university years (1981–85), when I began to ask the question, "Is this all there is to the Christian life?" I was still a babe in Christ, and I knew that God had released me from my sins, but I was still plagued with the flesh and all kinds of insecurities and hang-ups. I was (on the surface) doing well relationally, my education was moving ahead, and I even enjoyed being chosen class president my junior year. But inside, I felt empty, alone, and unsure of God's love and acceptance of me. In my mind, I was the loneliest-not-alone person there was.

It was about that time a roommate of mine introduced me to some material written by a church elder from Colorado named Miles Stanford. It was entitled *The Green Letters* series.[24] For the first time in my life, I began to understand more vividly

---

[24] Miles J. Stanford, *The Principles of Spiritual Growth* (Grand Rapids, MI: Zondervan, 1964; 1975), 20.

what exactly took place when Jesus redeemed me. When I began to read *The Green Letters* series, I was irresistibly drawn to its contents. The chief subject of "Not I, but Christ" was the main artery on my road to spiritual freedom. I soon began to get everything I could get my hands on that had to do with what has been erroneously called by many, even today, "Deeper Life" material. As I began to meditate on these particular teachings from the Newer Testament and apply them to my situation, I began to realize that these truths weren't just for "seasoned, mature Christians." They were foundational and really needed to be taught and understood from the very *start* of our Christian life and walk.

Over the thirty years of my Christian life and the twenty-plus years of my marriage, I have seen how knowing and appropriating my identity in Christ has made me a clear *victor* and no longer a pathetic *victim* in life. I have witnessed how it has kept me spiritually strong and produced consistent spiritual stability in my life. It is not just a theory; it is as practical as anything could possibly be.

Who in God's name are *you*? I hope, for the rest of your days, you can answer that question with what God has recorded in His word. The truth is all we have when we want to know the truth. Remember what we said. The choice is elementary. Either we will believe what others and/or our culture says about us, and I remind you, that is a dead-end street, or we will believe the God of the universe's record and His estimation of us. What you decide will make all the difference in this world and in the next! Cheers!

8

The Key to Freedom: Trading Lies for the Truth

"Who changed **the truth of God into a lie**, and worshipped and served the creature more than the Creator, who is blessed forever. Amen."

–Romans 1:25 [emphasis mine]

"For you are the children of your father the devil and you love to do the evil things he does. He was a murderer from the beginning. He has always hated the truth, because there is no truth in him. When he lies, it is consistent with his character; **for he is a liar and the father of lies.**"

–John 8:44 (NLT; emphasis mine)

Christopher Columbus was considered by most of his day to be out of his mind and was rejected and threatened with being slowly burned to death.

All because he believed the world wasn't flat, but round. Isn't that crazy? It is more bizarre when you realize that in 322 BC, Aristotle, a well-known Greek philosopher, also seemed to know that the world was round. Not only did the Greeks know that the world was spherical in shape, but in 240 BC, another Greek, Eratosthenes, accurately calculated the earth's diameter! So why, more than seventeen hundred years later, did a large chunk of civilization believe the earth was flat? Didn't they get the memo? The answer seems clear at least to me: If you repeat a lie often enough and long enough, people actually begin to believe it's the truth!

For thousands of years, the "Father of Lies, Satan" has propagated deception in a widespread manner. These deceptions are both grand and clever. In fact, he is at his best when he is lying and stealing from humanity. Mankind seems to smoothly and swiftly follow "the lie," and thereby, slowly slides into hell. Lies and truth are what make the world go around, and it is the child of God who is most affected by both.

In this chapter, we simply want to compare and contrast the destruction of believing the lies of Satan and the delight and freedom that comes from believing and living out God's truth. It's a pretty simple study, but you will not believe what you will learn in this chapter. It is a beautiful study to engage in.

Replacing Lies with Truth

The Christian life is all about trading or replacing old, crusty lies for God's relevant truth. When the

Bible tells us to "renew our minds" (Rom. 12:2), what it is saying is, trade the lies you have falsely believed with God's truth, which is wholly believable. Renew means to "make new" your understanding. Spiritual freedom and complete surrender (discipleship) is the goal of Christ for us. Listen to what Christ said from His own lips.

> Jesus said to the people who believed in him, "You are truly my disciples if you remain faithful to my teachings. And **you will know the truth, and the truth will set you free.**" "But we are descendants of Abraham," they said. "We have never been slaves to anyone. What do you mean, 'You will be set free'?" Jesus replied, "I tell you the truth, everyone who sins is a slave of sin. A slave is not a permanent member of the family, but a son is part of the family forever. **So if the Son sets you free, you are truly free**" (John 8:31–36, NLT; emphasis mine).

Paul wrote, **"It is for freedom that Christ has set us free.** Stand firm, then, and do not let yourselves be burdened again by a yoke of slavery" (Gal. 5:1, NIV; emphasis mine).

If the truth be told, Christ catches fire over us being free! He loves when we are released from the chains of sin and shame. That is why He came. That is why we need to continue our quest to be all that God wants us to be. Freedom is the song we must sing, the hope we must hold onto. It is our calling. Yes, the call of liberty is being made to you this day. *Will you answer that love call?*

The Father of Lies Revealed

Before we can fully understand the truth, we have to recognize lies. If we cannot tell the difference between the two, then how can we ever think that we will live enduring "real" lives? Truth is, we cannot, and we can never expect to enjoy the consistent smile of God or His peace, for that matter. This makes this chapter extremely important. Focus!

As we have discovered in this chapter, the Bible calls Satan (or the Devil) a liar and literally the inventor and Father of Lies (John 8:44). He is in his comfort zone when he is leading you and me into deception and dishonesty.

I read a story about Satan, who was on the side of life's road with a very large cage. A man coming towards him noticed that it was crammed full of people of every kind: young, old, and from every race and nation. "Where did you get these people?" the man asked. "Oh, from all over the world," Satan replied. "I lure them with drinking, drugs, lust, lies, anger, hate, love of money, and all manner of things. I pretend I'm their friend, out to give them a good time, then when I've hooked them, into the cage they go." "And what are you going to do with them now?" asked the man.

Satan grinned. "I'm going to prod them, provoke them, and get them to hate and destroy each other; I'll stir up racial hatred and defiance of law and order; I'll make people bored, lonely, dissatisfied, confused, and restless. It's easy. People will always listen to what I offer them and (what's better) they will blame God for the outcome!" "And then what?" the man asked. "Those who do not destroy themselves, I will destroy. None will escape me." The man stepped forward. "Can I buy these people from you?" he asked. Satan snarled, "Yes, but it will cost you your life." *Strike three!*

The great news is that Jesus Christ, the Son of God, paid for your release—your freedom from Satan's trap—with His own life on the cross. The door is open, and anyone whom Satan has deceived and caged can be set free. There is no reason to live in the shadows any longer. Did you hear that?

The Father of Truth Uncovered

If Satan is the Father of Lies (John 8:44), then it stands to reason that God is the father of truth. In the same way that there is no lie that does not have the Devil's fingerprints all over it, all spiritual truth is God's truth. The Scriptures have much to say about God being "truth."

For instance, in Matthew 22:16, Matthew writes, "And they sent their disciples to him, along with the Herodians, saying, 'Teacher, we know that you are true and teach the way of God *truthfully* [italics mine], and you do not care about anyone's opinion, for you are not swayed by appearances.'"

In John 1:14, speaking of Jesus, it says, "And the Word became flesh and dwelt among us, and we have seen his glory, glory as of the only Son from the Father, full of grace and *truth*" (ESV; italics mine).

John 1:17 reads, "For the law was given through Moses; grace and *truth* came through Jesus Christ (ESV; italics mine).

In John 14:6, Jesus says, "I am the way, and the *truth*, and the life. No one comes to the Father except through me (ESV; italics mine).

Ephesians 4:20–21 records, "But that is not the way you learned Christ assuming that you have heard about him and were taught in him, as the *truth* [italics mine] is in Jesus."

But not only is the Triune God (Father, Son, and Holy Spirit) *true* in their essence but also *all that they say* is true and trustworthy.

The Bible, which is God's very word to His own people and to the masses, is the truth because it comes from a God of truth (John 8:31–36; 16:13; 17:17; 18:37; Eph. 1:13; 6:14; 2 Thess. 2:10–13; 1 Tim. 2:4; 2 Tim. 2:15; 4:4; James 1:18; 1 John 1:6, 8).

We can be confident of one thing in this world. God is true, and if we follow His truth, then all will be well with us.

How Do We Believe the Truth of God and Reject the Lies?

In a moment we are going to go on a journey that I am willing to wager most of you have never been on. We do not easily learn to see lies and truth for what they are. If we are going to live in spiritual freedom and joy, we *must* learn to reject the lies of our enemy and swallow hook, line, and sinker the truths of God revealed in the Bible.

But how does this happen?

Well, it begins by first believing that you have consumed a buffet of lies in your earthly travels. Admit it. You and I have been saddled with so many lies from the cultural bath we have endured that it is a great miracle that we can receive or even believe any of God's truth. The shame of it is, we often are totally clueless to the fact that these lies are taking a tragic toll on us. So the first discovery we must make is that we are burdened down with a load of lies that will, in time, *destroy us!*

Next, we must believe that God's truth is much better and far greater for us in this life and the next. Unless we see the value of knowing God's truth and replacing the lies we have comfortably worn, we will never be changed into the image of Christ—and remember, that is God's desire for every last one of His children.

Notice the following insightful words: The folkish-minded man, in particular, has the sacred duty, each in his own denomination, of making people stop just talking superficially of God's will, and actually fulfill God's will, and not let God's word be desecrated. For God's will gave men their form, their essence, and their abilities. Anyone who destroys His work is declaring war on the Lord's creation, the divine will.

Pretty wise words for us as we consider exchanging lies for the will and truth of God. Who said these poignant words? Hold on to your hat. It was Adolph Hitler in *Mein Kampf*, volume 2, chapter 10.[25] Yikes!

I quoted this for a reason.

Most times, the lies we religious people believe are mixed in with a little truth, or they come from a person that is (in the dark) very dark themselves but often

---

25 Adolph Hitler, *Mein Kampf,* ed. Ralph Mannheim (New York: Mariner Books, 1999), 562.

maliciously plays the part of a saint or religious mentor. Isn't that true? We have all seen it. We must be so convinced that God's truth reigns supreme that we are willing to reject anything else that poses for the truth.

Finally, we must exchange lies for truth because Satan is the father and inventor of lies, and we do not want to walk in his footsteps! Do we? On our best day, we say, "No way will I follow Satan." On the days we are coaxed into believing that walking out the truth is negotiable–in Satan's footsteps we will go! But here's the deal. We know inwardly that our God wants us and bids us to learn of Him: He is the gateway to real truth. So we must pay the price to definitively deal with the comfortable deceptive clothes we have worn with pride for all of our lives. When, at the end of our lives, we are scanning the files of our days, we will do well (and be elated) if we have chosen the narrow road of following the will of God, no matter the cost.

So, with that said, strap in for an exhilarating ride. You are about to enter God's "no spin zone."

Trading Lies for God's Truth

Remember what we said at the beginning of our chapter: the key to spiritual freedom is found in casting out the lies of Satan and replacing them with the truth of God found in His Word, the Bible.

Let me show you how, as a child of God, you can trade the lies of the enemy for the truth of God on a continual basis. Remember, it is all about what your mind and heart will believe. Your feelings and the lies that you have cuddled up to over the years offer no spiritual help when it comes to spiritual freedom.

Don't take that statement lightly. Let's explode together the lies that we have been taught and have believed much of our life.

The Devil's Lie: "I can't do anything; I am powerless to live for God."

God's Truth: "I can do all things through Christ who gives me the strength" (Phil. 4:13).

The truth is that without Christ working *in* us and *through* us, we can do nothing of eternal significance. As we have seen throughout our first eight chapters, the Christian life and its power come from only *one* source—the Triune God (The Father, the Son, and the Holy Spirit). Of course, with Christ, Paul says (and he should know) all things are possible, and the strength to really live life on the highest plane is ours for the *asking* and the *believing*.

The Devil's Lie: "I am worthless. I am no good. I am a failure."

God's Truth: "I am God's masterpiece re-created in Christ Jesus (Eph. 2:10) . . . and I am more than a winner through Christ who loves me" (Rom. 8:37).

The truth is, you are what you may not believe yourself to be—in *Christ!* We grow up believing that we are no good or not good enough. Or that we are prone to failure, and because of that—we feel and believe ourselves to be without worth or value. When is last the time you looked in mirror and said, "In Christ, I am God's masterpiece. I am someone of great and important excellence"?

When is the last time you said to yourself, "I am a winner in Christ simply because He loves me"? You say, "That is not how I feel." There you go again. These truths from the mouth of the Holy Spirit are what the real deal is about for every true Christian, no matter how they act, feel, or even believe about themselves.

The Devil's Lie: "I cannot stand up against the Devil when he tempts me."

God's Truth: "Greater is He that is in me than he that is in the world" (1 John 4:4).

The Devil wants us to think that when temptation rears its ugly face, it's a massive flood that we have no way of avoiding or rising above. That is his lie, and often, we believe it. He also wants us to believe that it is "us against him" when it comes to the fight. It is not. The battle was waged and settled at the cross by the blood that Jesus shed (Col. 2:13–15; Heb. 2:14–15). Ephesians 6:10–18 says every believer must stand in the power of God's might against the enemy. John reminds us that the Holy Spirit in us is greater than any spiritual force outside of us (1 John 4:4). All these are our "truth tickets" to win in life on a daily basis.

The Devil's Lie: "I am a product of my past. I will never be able to become a whole person."

God's Truth: "If any person is in Christ, they are a new creation, all things are gone and new things have come" (2 Cor. 5:17).

One of the sweetest realities of having our sins forgiven is that we become entirely new people at the core of our being. Yes, we have a new destination that we will finally reach someday—*heaven*. We have new desires that from the beginning of our new life want to do right and shun evil. It may not wash out right away, but your old nature has been rendered powerless (Rom. 6:6), and you now have a "new nature" that desires to live for God and His kingdom (2 Pet. 1:4).

You are a new creation in Christ, which means you are not what you used to be spiritually and positionally. "And all these things are from God . . ." (2 Cor. 5:18).

The Devil's Lie: "I am gripped by fear in life and I cannot get over it."

God's Truth: "God has not given us a spirit of fear, but of power (strength to fight the fear), love (strength to melt the fear), and a sound mind (strength to replace the fear)."

Fear that paralyzes and imprisons is from the *enemy* of our souls—plain and simple. We have to stop justifying fear as a "normal, healthy" emotion because that is never what God does or says. In fact, in 2 Timothy 1:7, God goes so far as to call it a "spirit of fear"! Now, I ask you, if God is not the author of crippling fear, then guess who gets the prize? Satan and his demons are behind fear, and we must give no place to it in our lives as true Christians. This "spirit" God has been totally shattered in my own life in the last few years. I was truly unaware of its impeding impact, but the freer I become from fear, the more I recognized the grip it had on me—even as a minister of the good news. You may not think that fear is a root spirit in your life, but let God show you if that is true or not. You deserve to be free from fear once and for all.

The Devil's Lie: "I am dumb, unintelligent, and someone who can never be what others are."

God's Truth: "I have the mind of Christ (1 Cor. 2:16) and all the wisdom I need to make wise, godly decisions" (James 1:5).

Simply believing you are dumb or uneducated is to miss the point of God's wisdom entirely. Listen to what Paul said to the infantile Christian church at Corinth:

As the Scriptures say, "I will destroy the wisdom of the wise and discard the intelligence of the intelligent." So where does this leave the philosophers, the scholars, and the world's brilliant debaters? God has made the wisdom of this world look foolish. Since God in his wisdom saw to it that the world would never know him through human wisdom, he has used our foolish preaching to save those who believe. It is foolish to the Jews, who ask for signs from heaven. And it is foolish to the Greeks, who seek human wisdom. So when we preach that Christ was crucified, the Jews are offended and the Gentiles say it's all nonsense.

As a child of God, you have the mind of Christ (2 Cor. 2:16) and the wisdom of God. Is there really anything else you need? Why would you believe the lie that you are stupid and unintelligent when what counts in God's world is—are you filled and saturated with the divine thinking of God? Yes, you are. Case closed.

The Devil's Lie: "I feel so condemned and guilty about what I have done in the past."

God's Truth: "There is now – no condemnation or guilt to those who are in Christ Jesus" (Rom. 8:1).

Guilt in our lives is either real or a lie that we are believing. If we have come to know Christ in salvation, then guilt or eternal doom has been negated from the equation of our lives. True, targeted *conviction* comes from the Holy Spirit. *Guilt* comes ultimately from the "unholy spirit" or in the cheap, slick disguise of "false guilt." God has either freed you from your past and its shame or you are stuck in it forever, and that is simply not what the Holy Scriptures teach. "No guilt" is Paul's cry if we are God's children. If guilt is weighing you down, chide it and refuse its place in your life simply reminding yourself of the forgiveness of God for all that you have done—past, present, and future.

The Devil's Lie: "I feel so all alone, and it seems like no one loves or cares for me."

God's Truth: "Jesus said in Matthew 28 that He would be with us always, and He said that He would never leave us or forsake us" (Heb. 13:5).

So many of God's people suffer from loneliness and a feeling of not belonging. That is beyond sad because the truth is, we are in the palm of the hand that is the very essence of love and care. We can never, never, never (did I say *never*?) be separated from the love of Christ. Feelings of isolation and loneliness are just that—*feelings*. The truth is that you are not alone, and you are forever a part of the greatest family network in the universe—the family of God!

The Devil's Lie: "I feel so helpless when I am with others. I feel like I'm a real bother."

God's Truth: "If God is for me, who can be against me?" (Rom. 8:31).

Now you either are going to believe this or you will continue to party on in self-pity and defeat. Paul says it does not matter who is for me or against me. God is for me and that is enough.

I like what the psalmist wrote (or actually, sang) when he said, "If it had not been for the Lord who was on our side, where would we be?" That's for sure. But He is on our side even though we often are not on His. There is no reason for the child of God to feel helpless and defeated in this world. Jesus Christ graced a bloody cross so that you and I would not have to be helpless or hopeless in this world. Do not forget that

"We are more than winners through Him who loved us" (Rom. 8:37). Do not forget it!

The Devil's Lie: "God could never love me because of who I am or the bad things I have done."

God's Truth: "I have loved you with an everlasting love" (Jer. 33:3) and "His love was shown to us in while we were still sinners, Christ died for us" (Rom. 5:8).

This is another lie that seeks to circumvent the cross work of Christ. If I were to ask you what the chief quality (attribute) of God is, I wonder if you would say, "That's easy—love?" It's OK if you believe that, but love is really an outflow of God's complete and utter holiness! Because God is holy, the Bible says that He cannot even look upon sin (Hab. 1:13). Proof of this was what God the Father had to do to God the Son on the cross. Why do you think Jesus said at one point, "My God, my God, why have you forsaken Me?

Simply because He could not look or stand to gaze upon the sin of the entire world on the back of His one and only Son. That is why Jesus couldn't say, "My Father, My Father," because at that moment, Jesus became sin for us who knew no sin so that we might become the righteousness of God in Him (2 Cor. 5:21).

Now, all that to say this: If a God so holy and so overflowing with love, how do you even entertain the idea that He cannot or will not—love you? Romans 5:8 tells us that when we were at our *worst*, God's great and enduring love was at its *best*! If God never again showed us that He loved us, the cross would be enough for us. His love was poured out to overflowing there. It is where we are to measure His love for us the most in the dark days of our lives.

The Devil's Lie: "I am better than everyone else because I am a Christian."

God's Truth: "I am what I am by the grace of God" (1 Cor. 15:10).

One of the sad but real truths about Christians today is the fact that some, maybe many, feel that they are better than the lost crowd. That God certainly must love them more than those who regularly spit in God's face and professionally reject His word. No, not hardly! Now it's true God does love us *differently* as His children (just as we do on Earth), but His love holds no more intensity for us just because we are His kids! And Paul had it right when he in essence taught that the ground is level at the foot of the cross. We are what we are by God's grace, and it is good for us to realize that "there *we* go but for the grace of God." Don't ever forget it!

The Devil's Lie: "I am a victim of abuse; therefore, I will never be of any value to God or others."

God's Truth: "I am a saint (Eph. 1:1), I am chosen of God and dearly loved (Col. 3:12), and I am born of God and the evil one cannot touch me" (1 John 5:18).

If the identity driven life teaches us anything, it teaches us that our value is not in ourselves or in what we have accomplished or failed to accomplish. Our value lies in the cross and in the fact that we are "new creations in Christ." Satan loves to bring up our gory pasts. He loves to shame us—or keep us in shame—because he knows that this will keep us on the sidelines for "Team God." He is an accuser of the brothers and sisters, and he wants you to believe that your abuse was either your fault or was such that you could never rebound from it.

Well, I got news for you. He is a liar and the inventor of lies, and what Satan means for evil, God means for good so that Jesus Christ might be lifted up. Is abuse harmful? Of course it is. But it is not the end of a life, nor is it the "curse" that makes a child of God valueless to God or others. You are a saint of the living God, and because you are "born of God," the evil one can no longer play you like a play toy. So stop walking around like you are the grime beneath the toes of Jesus. Stand firm in the grace and love of Jesus Christ, which shouts to you from a bloodstained cross—*you are precious to me!*

The Devil's Lie: "I am not sure that God has everything in complete control."

God's Truth: "God sits in the heavens and does whatever pleases Him" (Ps. 115:3).

One of Satan's greatest strategies is to get us to believe that God isn't paying attention (or, at least, "full attention") to the details of our lives. That He is not aware of all that is happening in our lives and that the adversity we face is more like a penalty for our sloppy living. We begin to wonder what God is up to in our chaos and if He really cares all that much if we go down for the count! Well, according to God's word from Genesis to Revelation, I can confidently report to you that He *does* care and that He is in full and complete control of the world and *your* world! He sits in the heavens, says the psalmist, and does whatever pleases Him. That pretty much sums it up. He's God. He can do that, and He is more than accomplished to carry it out. Give God your life and all that is kicking around in it. He can do more with it than you can. The statement is true, "Little is much when God is in it." The lies are never-ending in this life, so let me toss out a few more and see how God answers back. It's really encouraging.

The Devil's Lie: "In order to get ahead in life, you must crush those in competition with you."

God Truth: "Humble yourself and take the form of a servant to really get ahead."

God's elevator functions this way: Up is *down* and down is *up*! Jesus said it plainly, "He who is first shall be last, and the last shall be first." Being a true follower of Christ means that you are more concerned with God's approval over and above man's approval. It means that you do not strive to beat and bury others so you can stand alone on a hill of your own foolish making. God's elevator surely is paradoxical. The way to succeed and prosper is to help others succeed and prosper. There is no other way to live.

The Devil wants you to believe that if you don't look out for yourself, then no one else will. We know that is a lie because the source of our life is not earthly, but *heavenly*. It is not to be found in man, but God. The one who owns all the cattle on a thousand hills and the wealth of every gold mine is the One who will take care of you if you will digest the simple teaching of Jesus that goes like this, "It is more blessed to give than to receive" (Acts 20:35).

The Devil's Lie: "Get all you can and can all you get in life."

God's Truth: "Give and it will be given to you. God's heavenly banking system says to save is to lose and to lose is to gain."

Jesus said on one occasion that a man's life is not found in the abundance of the things he possesses. In other words, the person who has the most toys at the end of life is nothing more than a person who has miserably failed to invest his heart and resources in God's investment firm. God wants us to be characterized as "givers," not "getters." He wants us to seek His kingdom first, and then we can expect that He will give us what we need when we need it (Matt. 6:33).

Invest in what is going to last. Not in things that will be left behind to who knows who when they throw dirt on you someday. Invest in people and their spiritual destinies. Invest in what cannot be ruined or stolen. Learn the secret of using things and loving people and not using people to romance things. God's heavenly banking system is firmly built on recklessly giving all that you are and have *away* so that God may get the glory!

The Devil's Lie: "I am rich because of what I have."

God's Truth: "You are rich because of who you are in My Son."

God's true riches are not material or tangible, but spiritual and eternal. True riches are spiritual and not material. Anyone can make money, save it, and see it multiply. There is nothing wrong with that, but we often make the mistake of allowing things to own us instead of us merely owning things. Our wealth is not in a bank vault or in the stock or foreign markets of the world, but they are to be found chiefly in the person and work of Jesus Christ. I believe it was C. S. Lewis who said, "He who has God and everything has no more than he who has God alone." It is always nice when God gives us *both*, but this desire is not necessarily the will of God for us. That is why Jesus talked so much about how our love for money and our love for God cannot be bosom buddies. We will love one and despise the other, or we will seek one and give lip service to the other. Even the church in Laodicea (Revelation 3) had the wrong measuring stick when it came to real riches. Remember what Jesus had to say to them.

> I know your works: you are neither cold nor hot. Would that you were either cold or hot! So, because you are lukewarm, and neither hot nor cold, I will spit you out of my mouth. **For you say, I am rich, I have prospered, and I need nothing, not realizing that you are wretched, pitiable, poor, blind, and naked. [Ouch!]** I counsel you to buy from me gold refined by fire, so that you may be rich, and white garments so that you may clothe yourself and the shame of your nakedness may not be seen, and salve to anoint your eyes, so that you may see. [emphasis mine]

True riches are in Christ, and false riches are anything that is trusted in *apart* from Christ!

The Devil's Lie: "In order to be strong, you must become self-sufficient and hard on the inside."

God's Truth: "In order to be strong, you must become weak."

God's strength in us is from Him, not in us that He might get all the credit. All of us seek to be strong for ourselves and others. We put a huge premium on being strong and tough in our society. Even as toddlers, we learn to stand up and refuse to let the winds of disappointment and adversity keep us down for good. That is good in itself, but it often replaces the real need to be "strong in the Lord." And you cannot (I said, you *cannot*) be strong in yourself and strong in the Lord at the same time.

The apostle Paul said it best in 2 Corinthians 12:7–10. Listen to his words about the place of strength and weakness in our Christian experience.

> So to keep me from becoming conceited because of the surpassing greatness of the revelations, a thorn was given me in the flesh, a messenger of Satan to harass me, to keep me from becoming conceited. Three times I pleaded with the Lord about this, that it should leave me. But he said to me, "My grace is sufficient for you, **for my power is made perfect in weakness.**" Therefore I will boast all the more gladly of my weaknesses, so that the power of Christ may rest upon me. For the sake of Christ, then, **I am content with weaknesses, insults, hardships, persecutions, and calamities. For when I am weak, then I am strong.** [emphasis mine]

God's power is perfected in our weakness. That's pretty sweet. That means that when we are in a position where we realize that we can do nothing apart from Christ, then God is able to supernaturally take up the slack. Paul was content [perfectly at ease and comfortable] with weakness and the position of need.

Why? Because Paul says when I am weak, something strangely wonderful happens—I become strong! Not strong in myself, but in Christ. Not weak in the Lord, but weak in myself. Do not buy into the Devil's lie anymore about strength and weakness. "He [Christ] must increase and you must decrease." There is no other way to sense and experience God's supernatural power in your life and ministry than this.

The Devil's Lie: "We are valuable and of worth because of what we do."

God's Truth: "What and who we are in Christ gives us value and worth."

God's value is measured in the Son He loves and what He accomplished on Calvary's cross. We as humans are very familiar with the word "do" but often are lacking in our understanding of the word "done." Do you remember one of the phrases that Jesus uttered on the cross as he was dying? "It is finished." Notice he did not say, "I am finished, but *it* [the work that the Father gave to me] is finished." Now, if I were to ask you, "Is there anything else that Jesus needs to "do" to secure salvation for us," what *would* you say? What *should* you say? The answer is simple: nothing! The Scriptures are clear on this matter. Jesus, through His sacrificial death and glorious resurrection, accomplished *everything* that mankind would ever need to be one with God forever. There is nothing more to "do" because all of it has been "done." Are you with me?

Question: Is your value as a "new creation in Christ" (2 Cor. 5:17; Eph. 2:10) dependent on you or God?

Well, we can ask, "What have we 'done' by our own merits to receive this great value and worth?" Remember that the image that we were made in has been horribly marred but the dark stain of sin? There are only two possible conclusions to this. Either our eternal salvation and infinite worth and value to God is based on what we "do or have done" or it is found solely in the person and work of Jesus Christ in which he declared once and for all—**"done!"** I think you know the answer here as well. If the Devil can keep you caged in the "lie" that you are valuable because of who you are and what you do, then you will never be free to live and serve Christ joyfully!

God's value of us is measured in the Son He loves and what He accomplished on Calvary's cross. That's it, but thanks be to God, that is more than enough! *Rest* in that today. You don't have to try to figure it all out. It is what it is. Rejoice in its fact!

The Devil's Lie: "In order to really live, you must live it up because you only go around one time."

God's Truth: "In order to really live, you must die to self."

God's life is found in knowing we have died with Christ in order that we might live in and with Him.

"Eat, drink, and be merry, for tomorrow we die" is an old phrase that actually has biblical roots. In fact, the apostle Paul told the church at Corinth that if the resurrection of Jesus was a sham and unreal, then to live it up with no restraints was the way to go in this life (1 Cor. 15:32). Most people think that you only live "once" so on your trip, you might as well get all you can and can all you get. The philosophy "He who owns the most toys at the end of life—wins" is espoused by most of the developed countries of the world, but remember Jesus said that a person's life does not consist or matter based on how much they have or own. The Scriptures say that if we are going to really live, we must really *die!* We must die to our own pursuits, our own treasured dreams, and to everything that squeezes God out of first position in our lives (Luke 9:23–25). God's life is active and real when we deeply know we have died with Christ in order that we might live in and with Him.

Now, then . . .

All these lies from Satan and all these biblical truths are what make us who we are. We must understand that God's ways are not our ways, much less the culture's ways. It is all about having a "God's kingdom mindset." We have to understand that God's rule is an "upside down" rule, and what seems to be natural to us must be replaced with the supernatural.

The Perfect Marriage of Identity and Purpose

Make a note of this: the carriage was never meant to lead the horse. It doesn't work, and besides, it is a moronic way to operate.

The identity message is a message that always comes before the purpose message. I hope that in the course of this book, I have established in your mind that essential truth. You can never fully know your purpose for living if you fail to calculate who you are while you live. I have repeatedly hammered this truth home—to the tune of annoyance, I know. Yet, its truth cannot just be yawned over, and I'm afraid it has been for far too long.

Let me say this so there is no misunderstanding. Knowing your purpose is vital if you are going to be used of God in a way He desires. Knowing your purpose in life is the key to being able to carry out the great things and works that God has designed for us to use. This isn't a "choose one or the other" proposition.

Just as *The Purpose Driven Life* was designed to be a "textbook" on knowing your purpose, it is my desire as well to make this book so "user-friendly" when it comes to identity that is serves the selfsame purpose!

In fact, I would go a step further. *The Identity Driven Life* is really a companion to *The Purpose Driven Life*. They fit nicely together, in this writer's opinion. They each occupy a side of the coin that can be spiritually received and cashed in for the glory of God. Both are needed if we are to be all that God wants us to be, and I hope that is what you want. But let me be clear. I am fully convinced that knowing your purpose **cannot** be fully operational unless you first know and live out your spiritual identity. That might explain a lot of the frenzied activity we see in many church people and the lack of true Christian character that must be the support and *propel* the activity.

Dr. Tony Evans, pastor and author of many bestselling books, writes something in his book *Free At Last* that made me sit up in my recliner. Maybe it shouldn't have, but it did. A respected pastor and speaker, Evans has preached many, many sermons in his lifetime. He has equally spoken on a myriad of subjects in his pursuit to build up the church and the child of God. With all that said, here is what he said about the great worth of knowing and receiving our identity in Christ.

"I consider the truth about our identity in Christ to be the greatest principle of Christian living in Scripture."[26] Wow! That is quite a statement. There is no greater essential truth in the New Testament that the child of God needs to grasp than their lofty and prized position in Christ. It is the very *foundation* of the Christian

[26] Tony Evans, *Free at Last* (Chicago: Moody Press, 2001), 12.

faith, and it is theme of the whole New Testament writings, at least from Romans to Revelation.

Romans 8:28–32— Identity and Purpose Entangled

Romans 8, verses 28 through 32, pass on to us the excellent friendship that divine identity and purpose really share. Notice what the Holy Spirit says to us:

> And we know that in all things God works for the good of those who love him, who have been called according to his purpose. For those God foreknew he also predestined to be conformed to the image of his Son, that he might be the firstborn among many brothers and sisters. And those he predestined, he also called; those he called, he also justified; those he justified, he also glorified. What, then, shall we say in response to these things? If God is for us, who can be against us? He who did not spare his own Son, but gave him up for us all—how will he not also, along with him, graciously give us all things? (NLT)

I want you to notice the last part of verse 28: "who have been called according to His purpose. . . ."

We have already established that to be "called" is another way of saying our identity or position in Christ. *Calling*, Paul says in Romans 8:28, comes *before* purpose.

In verse 29, Paul says something more about identity and purpose when he says that God knew ahead of time that He was going to call us, not based on anything that we have done, but only on His all-knowing capabilities. And what was His calling and predetermined desire for us as His children? "To be conformed (shaped or molded) to the image (likeness) of God's Son, Jesus." Ah, there it is! Paul wanted the Roman Christians to know (and us, as well, today) that the Christian life from start to finish is not us becoming a better version of ourselves but us becoming a living version of the life of Christ within us. There is a great difference in the two, you know.

Then, in verse 30, Paul drives the point of identity before purpose home when he reminds us that for those God prearranged to be saved, His work was in this order: called, justified, glorified. When Paul had a chance to expound on this great salvation that we have been recipients of, he keeps it simple and focused. Salvation before service—period!

Knowing our salvation and the calling we enjoy spurs us to a greater, weightier service than we could ever know and experience if we only simply know our "purpose!" Do we need to know the divine purpose God has for us in this life? Absolutely! Without knowing it, we will wander around like the Israelites did in the wilderness. Yet, the order is essential to see not only from the whole of the New Testament but also from Paul's words here in Romans 8.

Paul, like any good preacher, stops and poses a logical, makes-all-the-sense-in-the-world, question. "What, then, shall we say in response to these things?" We might say our God is awesome and great, and we would be right. We could be led to a shout of great praise to Jesus, and that would certainly be appropriate. But Paul says something that celebrates what we are trying to establish in this chapter. He says three things in verses 31 and 32 that I want you to see.

First, if God is for us, who could ever be against us. Think about that one for a minute (or a year, for that matter). Some of us (right now) can't get past the fact that it says, "God is for us." Why? My guess is it is probably because many of us have been taught and trained to believe that God is somewhat and in some way—mostly *against* us. Let's face the facts. Our sinful hearts and our daily conduct seem to scream to us that God must be mad, or at the very least, "disappointed" with us. The only thing that I can say to that is if you ever truly understand your identity and position in Christ, you will never seriously entertain that foolish thinking again! Sure God is against us before we know His Son, Christ. Yes, our sinful nature and our deeds of sin will cause us to perish eternally if we are not released from them. But we as God's children are no longer under the Old Covenant curse that condemns sin in the flesh. We are under grace (Rom. 6:14), and because we are, God is ever for us as His children–*one* question asked! Here's the question.

Is God ever "against" His children? *Yes,* he can be, Peter says. *When they are filled with pride.* "God **opposes** the proud but shows favor to the humble." (1 Pet. 5:5, NIV; emphasis mine). That is pretty heavy, but it is where God must draw the line. But that is the only place in the New Testament that challenges and alters what Paul says in Romans 8.

Second, Paul says, "He who did not spare his own Son, but gave him up for us all. . . ." What does that mean? It means that for us and on our behalf, God the Father chose not to spare God His one and only Son so we could experience true salvation from our sin and ourselves. He gave Him up for all of us. He did not have to.

He chose to.

Someone wisely said it was not the nails and the wood that held Jesus on the cross; it was His love that held him there. Nothing could be truer than that statement. He paid a (sin) debt that He didn't owe because we had a (sin) debt that we could never, in a trillion life times, pay. When Jesus cried out on the cross to His Father on why he was being forsaken of the Father, it must have torn the heart out of God. Jesus could have called thousands of angels to His rescue, but in the stunning plan of God, Jesus became like us—that we might become someday like Him. It doesn't get any better than that!

Finally, Paul reminds us, "how will he not also, along with him, graciously give us all things?" The good news concerning our identity in Christ is that "in Christ," we have all that we need to live for God in a pleasing manner. Paul reasons that if God did not spare Christ on the cross, then what we have in Christ is everything we need to serve Christ. And notice, in Christ, God gives us by His grace all things. Not some things spiritually speaking, but *all* things. Paul would later echo this same truth to the Ephesian church when he wrote, "All praise to God, the Father of our Lord Jesus Christ, who has blessed us with every **spiritual blessing** in the heavenly realms because we are united with Christ" (Eph. 1:3 NLT; emphasis mine).

William Newell, in his classic commentary on Romans, writes these penetrating words that drive home this truth perfectly:

> There being no cause in the creature why grace should be shown; the creature must be brought off from trying to give cause to God for His care. "He has been accepted in Christ, who is his standing!" "He is not on probation." "As to his life past, it does not exist before God: he died at the cross, and Christ is his Life." "Grace, once bestowed, is not withdrawn: for God knew all the human exigencies beforehand: His action was independent of them, not dependent upon them."
>
> To believe, and to consent to be loved while unworthy, is the great secret. To refuse to make "resolutions" and "vows"; for that is to trust in the flesh. To expect to be blessed, though realizing more and more lack of worth. To rely on God's chastening (child training) hand as a mark of His kindness. To "hope to be better" (hence acceptable) is to fail to see yourself in Christ only. To be disappointed with yourself is to have believed in yourself. To be discouraged is unbelief—as to God's purpose and plan of blessing for you. To be proud, is to be blind! For we have no standing before God, in ourselves. The lack of Divine blessing, therefore, comes from unbelief, and not from failure of devotion. **To preach devotion first, and blessing second, is**

to reverse God's order, and preach law, not grace
[emphasis mine]. The Law made man's blessing
depend on devotion; Grace confers undeserved,
unconditional blessing: our devotion may follow,
but does not always do so–in proper measure.[27]

You may want to read that paragraph again—and
again. It really does disclose the "real deal" when we
talk about the grace of God. The grace of God really
is a higher standard than even the law because while
we could do nothing to keep the law or receive life
from its commands, grace offers the believing sinner
the wonderful way to grow and not merely groan in
this life.

God has chosen, in this age of grace, to bless every
true believer in Jesus Christ on the *front-end*, not on
the back-end. Don't miss what I just wrote. Read that
last sentence again. It is no secret to the student of
Scripture that the law motivated people to do and
obey to be blessed of God. That is the theme of the
Old Covenant. But grace, according to John 1:17, was
introduced and made usable by Jesus Christ. Aren't
you glad that you do not have to perform *for* God
to be accepted *by* God? As someone said, "The law
condemns the best of us, yes, but the grace of Christ
redeems the worst of us." Praise His great name!

A true story is told of a millionaire who had a
portrait of his beloved son painted before the son
went to war. He was tragically killed in battle, and
shortly afterward, the heartbroken millionaire died.
His will stated that all his riches were to be auctioned,

---

[27] Newell, *Romans: Verse by Verse*, 201–02.

specifying that the painting must sell first. Many showed up at the auction, where a mass of the rich man's wealth was displayed. When the painting was held up for sale, there were no bids made. It was an unknown painting by an unknown painter of the rich man's uncelebrated son, so sadly, there was little interest. After a few moments, a butler who worked for the man remembered how much the millionaire loved his son, decided to bid for the portrait, and purchased it for a very low price. Suddenly, to everyone's surprise, the auctioneer brought down his gavel and declared the auction closed. The rich man's will had secretly specified that the person who cared enough to purchase the painting of his beloved son was also to be given all the riches of his will.

This is precisely what God has done through the good news of the gospel. He who accepts the beloved Son of Almighty God also receives all the riches of His will—"the gift of eternal life" and "pleasures for evermore." They literally become heirs of the Father and "joint heirs" with the Son (Rom. 8:16–17). O happy day!

And that, my friend, is the whole truth, nothing but the truth—*with the help of God*!

Identity Truth #2

You Are Unconditionally Loved By the One Who Counts

9

The Unconditional Love of God

"Nothing binds me to my Lord like a strong belief in His changeless love."

–Charles. H. Spurgeon[28]

"God loves each one of us as if there were only one of us to love."

–Saint Augustine[29]

God's great love for us can only be believed on and enjoyed; it can never fully be understood.

I once heard a story about a very rich but unhappy king. He was unhappy because he was all alone in an empty palace. How he longed for a wife with whom he could

---

[28] "Charles Spurgeon," *Christ Alone*, http://www.christalone. com/quote/170-charles-spurgeon?start=2.
[29] "Saint Augustine Quotes," *BrainyQuote*, http://www.brainy-quote.com/quotes/quotes/s/saintaugus105351.html.

share his life. Then, one day, the king saw the most beautiful woman he had ever seen, riding through the streets. We he inquired about her, he learned that she was a peasant girl, but the king's heart was captivated nonetheless. In fact, he rode past her house every day in the hope of catching a glimpse of this peasant girl.

But the king had a problem. *How would he win her love?* He certainly could draw up a royal decree commanding her to become his queen, but then he could never be sure he had won her love or that she was only with him because she was compelled to obey a royal decree. Perhaps he could call on her and try to win her over by appearing in all his regal glory, thereby sweeping her off her feet, but then he would never be sure whether she had married him only for his power and riches or because she truly loved him.

Finally, he came up with the perfect plan. He would come to her as a peasant. That was the only way he believed he could truly win her love. So he abandoned his palace and his riches and his comfort, and he put on the clothes of a peasant. He went and lived among the peasants. He worked with them, shared their sufferings, and danced at their feasts until he finally won the heart of the woman who had captured his.

So it is with God. Christ became one of us, lived among us, worked among us, suffered with us, and danced with us. All in order to win our hearts.

I want to discuss the unconditional, unwavering, unalterable love of Almighty God towards the world, and specifically, towards His kids. It is a monumental discussion that will leave you changed and challenged, I promise you.

First John 4:17 states, "God is love." But what does that mean, really? Do you believe God loves you no matter what? Do you believe His love for you is unconditional (no strings attached)?

False Ways of Measuring God's Love

We humans make a living out of making God out to be something He is *not*. Because of our limited knowledge and our often blurred spiritual vision, we bring God down to our level and even *below* our level if we're keeping it real. In our life, God morphs into a kind of glorified server who is demanded around by us, expected to wait on us like no one else exists. We, early in our relationship with God, still seek to assume the reigns of leadership that we handed over at salvation, all the while treating Him as if He still owes us something. We often expect from Him what should not be expected. We are happy when He answers our finger snapping and grouchy when He seems to ignore it. We often measure His love for us in very wrong and mistaken ways. Let me share a few with you and see if they ring true in your life.

False Way #1: God Loves Me by the Circumstances of My Life

We are prone to measure God's love toward us through the things that He either sends or allows in our lives. We certainly buy the idea that God's love is active towards us when all seems to be well, but when trouble, heartache, or deep disappointment knock on our door, we are then tempted and almost programmed to believe that God certainly cannot be happy with us.

That His love for us has changed, or at the very least, lessened in its intensity. I have one question: Where did we ever get that idea? Not from the Bible. I will prove it to you in a few minutes. Stay tuned.

False Way #2: God Loves Me When He Does What I Ask of Him

How many of us have come to believe this mixed-up reasoning? Sorry if you belong to the club (I did for a lot of years), but that kind of thinking is one of the chief reasons why many who call themselves "children of God" are stuck in their relationship with God and are constantly "stewing" over what God has failed to do in their life. The "God is my personal server" mentality has infected the church like a plague, and all the while, it makes the Devil a happy spirit. One question: Could it be that God's love has nothing to do with what we ask of Him or of what He asks of us? Just asking.

False Way #3: God Loves Me by What I Do and He Doesn't Love Me as Much if I Fail to Do What He Wants Me to Do

This idea that our works or performance has anything to do with God loving us (or loving us more) can plainly be defined as good old-fashioned "legalism"! If His love is dependent on what we do or fail to do, we would surely be on the losing end most of the time. And here's something to think about: How much work or service do we have to perform for His love to be strong in our lives? There is simply no way to know, but thank God we don't have to guess! Why? Because His love is real *despite* anything we can do or fail to do.

False Way #4: God's Love for Me Is as Strong as What I Have Been Taught

I believe that false beliefs rooted in our past and carried into the present are the greatest single reason why we doubt or fail to bathe in God's love. Listen: Very often, our "filter" or location point for the Father's love for us is the kind of earthly love our earthly fathers showed us. Don't miss that. So the million dollar question is: What does the Bible say about God's love for us. Remember, we cannot believe God any more than we believe His word, the Bible. Our feelings and circumstances are weak measures of what God truly thinks and feels about us. Life has certainly taught us that.

Remember—Identity Truth #2 says you are unconditionally loved by the One who really counts!

I truly believe that if we do not believe, receive, and live out the unconditional love God has for us, we will not grow, succeed, or become what God wants us to be. Additionally, we will not be able to receive rewards when we stand at the judgment seat of Christ. Pretty serious stuff, wouldn't you agree? So what we are discussing in this chapter is tremendously important. It is no time to brush it aside. Why? Because it will affect how we live here on Earth and how we fare on our final test before Christ on *that* day.

The Bible is clear on the matter of God's love for us. There are at least 254 references in the Bible about His love for His people. God always repeats His truth for a distinct reason. The Bible calls God and His *nature* love (1 John 4:8). He cannot *not* love people. It is the air He breathes. God is our Father, and it is the calling and responsibility of a father to love (Heb. 12:3–12). God has given us the same opportunity to love others as he has loved us (John 15:13; Rom. 5:5; Gal. 5:22). In other words, Christ desires to love others through us with His love, which is, by the way, unconditional and not self-serving.

What Does the Bible Say about God's Love toward Us?

As I said before, there is simply no way to rate or test God's love more than believing what the Old and New Testament say about it. Feeling His love or believing He loves me cannot be determined by my circumstances or my response to my surroundings. What we believe about God is revealed in Scripture, and we must believe or we will be forced to judge God out of our grid and that, most times, will not be pretty! Let the Scriptures speak to you in the next few minutes. Don't just speed past these. Digest them, for they are life to your soul. Read them more than once and believe and receive them.

Remember this about God's love:

1. It is unconditional and never ending. Jeremiah 31:3 states, "The LORD appeared to us in the past, saying: "I have loved you with an *everlasting love*; I have drawn you with unfailing kindness'"(NIV; italics mine). Romans 5:8 says, "but God shows *his love for us in that while we were still sinners*, Christ died for us" (ESV; italics mine).

If He loved us when we were at our *worst*, how will His love ever fail us when we are now a part of His family?

2. It is reliable and unfailing. (Count on it—no matter what.) Exodus 34:6 says, "The LORD, the LORD, the compassionate and gracious God, slow to anger, abounding in *love and faithfulness*" (NIV; italics mine). First Chronicles 16:34 reminds us to "Oh give thanks to the LORD, for he is good; for his *steadfast love* endures forever!" (ESV; italics mine).

If God's love for us is unfailing and sure, then why do we ever doubt it or question it?

3. It is indescribable. (We cannot adequately describe or define it.) Ephesians 3:18–19 notes, "may you have the power to understand, as all God's people should, how wide, how long, how high, and how deep his love is. May you experience *the love of Christ, though it is too great to understand fully.* Then you will be made complete with all the fullness of life and power that comes from God" (NLT; italics mine).

Since God's love for us in Christ is too great to understand fully, then stop trying to understand it! Instead, rest in it. Let it pour over you. Not because you deserve it, but because He dispenses it freely! Praise His great name!

4. It is wonderful (full of wonder and awe). Psalm 31:21 says, "Praise the LORD, for he has shown me the *wonders of his unfailing love.* He kept me safe when my city was under attack" (NIV; italics mine).

When the enemy comes in like a flood, the God of love is faithful to the core! We use the word "wonderful" for just about everything. God uses it for very few things. One of the uses is for—His love. His love is that to "wonder" over. That means take some time to think and envision it! Good times.

5. It is redeeming (willing to buy mankind back from the slave market of sin and ruin). Says Isaiah 63:9: "In all their distress he too was distressed, and the angel of his presence saved them" (ESV).

"In his love and mercy he redeemed them; he lifted them up and carried them all the days of old" (NIV; italics mine). Galatians 2:20 says, "Christ loved me (and you) and *gave Himself up for me* [italics mine] (and you)." God's love is a love that goes into the ghetto of sin and buys back the lost and weary. It is a sacrificial love, to be sure.

6. It is abundant (more than enough for us). Ephesians 2:3 says, "All of us also lived among them at one time, gratifying the cravings of our flesh and following its desires and thoughts. Like the rest, we were by nature deserving of wrath. But because of *his great love for us*, God, who is rich in mercy, made us alive with Christ even when we were dead in transgressions—it is by grace you have been saved" (NIV; italics mine). Romans 5:5 states, *"God's love has been poured out* in our hearts through the Holy Spirit who has been given to us" (NIV; italics mine).

God's love towards us is not just a trickle or a capful, but it comes to us in an overflowing, pour-it-on manner. That is the way God does things, you know? How long is the Holy Spirit with us? *Forever.* How long is God's love with us if it is joined by the Holy Spirit? *Forever.*

7. It is great. Says 1 John 3:1: "See what [an incredible] quality of love the Father has given (shown, bestowed on) us, that we should [be permitted to] be named and called and counted the children of God! And so we are!" (AMP).

The love of Christ is incredible and great not only because of whom He is but also because of whom we are in Him. Children of God, part of the King's family. We belong and it is all because of love.

8. It is full of forgiveness. In Zephaniah 3:17, it says, "For the Lord your God is living among you. He is a mighty savior. He will take delight in you with gladness. *With his love, he will calm all your fears. He will rejoice over you with joyful songs*" (NLT; italics mine).

Can you imagine the mighty Creator of all things smiling over you and singing to you? Hard to believe isn't it? Yet, it is true. If you get a charge out of singing lullabies to your little ones, you can relate to the fact that *God loves to sing lullabies to His children.* That ought to make you think twice about how He feels about you.

9. It is a constant companion. (It can never be absent in the child of God's life or situation.) Think about Romans 8:35–39:

Can anything ever separate us from Christ's love? Does it mean he no longer loves us if we have trouble or calamity, or are persecuted, or hungry, or destitute, or in danger, or threatened with death? (As the Scriptures say, "For your sake we are killed every day; we are being slaughtered like sheep.") No, despite all these things, overwhelming victory is ours through Christ, who loved us. *And I am convinced that nothing can ever separate us from God's love.* Neither death nor life, neither angels nor demons, neither our fears for today nor our worries about tomorrow—not even the powers of hell can separate us from God's love. No power in the sky above or in the earth below—indeed, nothing in all creation will ever be able to separate us from the love of God that is revealed in Christ Jesus our Lord (NLT; italics mine).

You can never go where God's love is not there first. It is in you, around you, beside you, and over you. Once again, His love has nothing to do with your behavior. It is a gift given by Christ because you are His and He is yours. Take a moment to "smile" over such a deep reality.

10. It motivates us to win over sin. (It gives us a winning attitude that leads us to a winning work.) Remember Romans 8:37: "No, despite all these things, overwhelming victory is ours *through Christ, who loved us* (NLT; italics mine).

God's love in Christ makes us present victors and defeats the "victim" mentality in our lives. Paul just doesn't say that we have victory. It isn't a 3-2 nail biter. It is an overwhelming crush or defeat of our enemy. His love pushes back and away all discouragement and defeat in our lives. We must stand in its reality, or it will not be reality for us, I'm afraid.

11. It is a fortress to run under. (His love is what we can live in moment by moment—no questions asked!) In Jude 1:20–21, it says, "But you, dear friends, must build each other up in your most holy faith, pray in the power of the Holy Spirit, and await the mercy of our Lord Jesus Christ, who will bring you eternal life. *In this way, you will keep yourselves safe in God's love* (NLT; italics mine).

In God's love there is complete safety and security. Safety is never the absence of fear lurking, but it is characterized by the presence of God and His steadfast love.

12. It is selfless and giving. John 15:13 says, *"Greater love* [italics mine] has no one than this that someone lay down his life for his friends."

Question: When we were in our sins, were we His *friends* or His *enemies*? According to Romans 5:6, 10, we were His avowed "enemies."

First John 3:16 puts it this way: "This is how *we know what love is*: Jesus Christ laid down his life for us. And we ought to lay down our lives for our brothers and sisters" (NIV; italics mine).

So, let's review and reason this out.

I ask you, if God's love is (according to the Scriptures that cannot lie) never-ending, reliable and unfailing, indescribable, wonderful and redeeming, abundant and great, full of forgiveness, a constant companion, motivating us to win in life, a fortress to run under, and selfless and ever-giving, then

- Why do we try to earn God's love as His child?
- Why do we ever doubt it?
- Why would we ever reject or not receive it fully?
- Why would we not live in light of all day and every day?
- Why do we believe the Devil when he says that God's love is probationary?

When you know all this about God and how He feels about you, does it really matter all that much what *others* think of you?

The Chief Way of Measuring God's Great Love

First, we understand God's love by what God's word says about us concerning His love toward us. God is not a man that He should lie. What He says, the Scriptures say, "is settled in heaven."

I close this chapter with the second and crowning reason on why we can believe that God, in Christ, has forever loved us and will continue to love us—no matter what.

How else can we measure the true love of God for us? By what God did for us thru the cross work of His Son.

The cross that Jesus died on conveys the simple but profound message, "I love you" for all time, but . . . only those who believe and receive the cross's message can expect to know, feel, and live in this eternal and unrestricted love. Did you get that? How do I know that? Look at the following verses:

> For God so loved the world that he gave his one and only Son, that whoever believes in him shall not perish but have eternal life. For God did not send his Son into the world to condemn the world, but to save the world through him. Whoever believes in him is not condemned, but whoever does not believe stands condemned already because they have not believed in the name of God's one and only Son. (John 3:16–18, NIV)

Dear friends, let us continue to love one another, for love comes from God. Anyone who loves is a child of God and knows God. But anyone who does not love does not know God, for God is love. God showed how much he loved us by sending his one and only Son into the world so that we might have eternal life through him. This is really *loved*—not that we loved God, but that he loved us and sent his Son as a sacrifice to take away our sins. (1 John 4:7–10, NIV; italics mine)

The cross is the exclamation point on what the Scriptures say about God's amazing love! You want to know if or how much God loves you in Christ? Just be brave enough to glance at the cross.

What Does the Cross of Christ Tell Me about God's Love?

Now the question is, what is the major *barricade* to receiving and living out God's love?

The answer to me is clear. **It is the belief and real feelings of rejection and self-condemnation!**

Someone relayed a story about a girl who was placed in an orphanage. She was unattractive and had mannerisms that were not very attractive either, so she was disliked and shunned by the other children and was not liked by her teachers. The head of the institution looked for a reason to send her off to some other place. One afternoon the opportunity came. She was suspected of writing unapproved, illicit notes to someone outside the institution. One of the little girls had just reported, "I saw her write a note and hide it on a tree near the stone wall." The superintendent hurried to the tree and found the note. He then passed it silently to his assistant. The note read, "To whoever finds this, I love you."

In essence, someone else also wrote a note and put it on a tree outside a city wall at another place a long time ago. Of him, too, it was written, "He had no beauty or majesty to attract us to him, nothing in his appearance that we should desire him. He was despised and rejected by men" (Isa. 53:2–3, NIV). They sought to get rid of Jesus. They took him out to Calvary's hill where they crucified him. They nailed him to a tree. But when men get there, they find a note on that tree that reads, "To whoever finds this, I love you."[30]

You will never fully **enjoy**; you will never fully **live out**; and you will never fully **give out** God's love *unless* you can come to the point that you realize you can . . . never do anything to earn God's love and you can never do anything to keep it! Your spiritual identity is this: you are unconditionally loved by the one who really matters. The question remains: will you believe what God says in His word about how He feels about you or will you continue to feed on the lies that have been planted in your heart by the enemy of your soul? There are only two choices. Both of them lead you down a road that will affect your life now and forever.

[30] Davon Huss, "To Whoever Finds This . . . I Love You," *Sermon Central*, http://www.sermoncentral.com/illustrations/sermon-illustration-davon-huss-stories-children-child-kids-82465.asp.

10

Abba Father Love–Yes!

"Father! To God himself we cannot give a holier name."

—William Wordsworth[31]

"The highest science, the loftiest speculation, the mightiest philosophy, which can ever engage the attention of a child of God, is the name, the nature, the person, the work, the doings, and the existence of the great God whom he calls Father."

—J. I. Packer[32]

It doesn't take as much to be a father as it takes to be a daddy.

Erma Bombeck, in her usual humorous way, wrote the following about fathers. "When I was a kid a father

---

[31] "Inspirational Quotes," *Beliefnet,* http://www.beliefnet.com/ Quotes/Christian/W/William-Wordsworth/Father-To-God- Himself-We-Cannot-Give-A-Holier-N.aspx.

[32] J. I. Packer, *Knowing God* (London: Hodder & Stoughton Ltd.-Hachette, 1973), n.p.

was like a light in the refrigerator. Everybody's house had one, but no one really knew what either of them did when the door was shut."[33]

Unlikeearthlyfatherswhohavealotofshortcomings, God finds no equal or challenger when it comes to His Fatherhood. He is who He is. The Father of all who call on His Name for a place in the family. But for us to allow Him the great privilege and passion to be a "dad" to us, well, that is an entirely different matter. Wish it wasn't, but it is, so the question is: What do we do about it? How do we swing wide open the door of our hearts so that God can be the dad we have never known? Let's talk about it.

Dr. J. I. Packer was—and *is*—a great theologian and writer. He wrote a book many years ago that was unquestionably celebrated far and wide in the Christian community. *Knowing God* was a landmark book that trumpeted the intimacy of Father God toward His children. Though Packer looked at many different attributes of God in his book, my favorite chapter (and one that made a tremendous impact in my life) was the one on "The Fatherhood of God." Weigh his words carefully:

> You sum up the whole of the New Testament teaching in a single phrase, if you speak of it as a revelation of the Fatherhood of the holy Creator. In the same way, you sum up the whole of New Testament religion if you describe it as the knowledge of God as one's Holy Father. If you

[33] Erma Bombeck, "The Daddy Doll Under the Bed," Newsday Newspaper Syndicate, June 21, 1981. Her column was entitled "At Wit's End."

want to judge how well a person understands Christianity, find out how much he makes of the thought of being God's child, and having God as his Father. If this is not the thought that prompts and controls his worship and prayers and his whole outlook on life, it means he does not understand Christianity very well at all. For everything that Christ taught, everything that makes the New Testament new, and better than the Old, everything that is distinctively Christian as opposed to merely Jewish is summed up in the knowledge of the Fatherhood of God. Father is the Christian name for God. **'Father' is the Christian name for God** [emphasis mine].[34]

That, at least to me, is a profound way of saying this. Let me say it this way.

Understanding our true identity in Christ begins with an honest assessment of who God exactly is. Read it again.

Now, God is a lot of things, to be sure, and His person is really past our ability to fully understand, but in talking about all the grand and great truths about the greatness and the loftiness of God, there stands a heartwarming and emotionally charged biblical portrait of God. This portrait, if we are not careful, will be overlooked, unappreciated, and in the end, ignored. If it is, we will run the race that God has set before us empty, discouraged, and emotionally and spiritually detached from the kind of life that God intended when He made us.

[34] Packer, *Knowing God*, n.p.

We welcome this portrait's entrance into our lives, but its entrance is a rough and difficult one. It is mainly because so many of us are so scarred from our early years and from the decisions that we have made apart from the wisdom of God in our adult life. This is pretty heavy language, but I'm just keeping it real. We have the love of God neatly stored in our cranium, but it is often a distant stranger at the core of our being. There is definitely an "eighteen-inch" difference in our understanding (the distance between the head and the heart). This portrait that needs to be hung on every heart is **the truth of God as our heavenly Dad!** Without it, we can never become the child of God that God desires and longs for us to be. And that is tragic!

Romans 8:15–17

One of the great Newer Testament verses on the intimacy of God as "heavenly Dad" is found in Romans 8, verses 15 through 17. I love how the Message paraphrases it:

> This resurrection life you received from God is not a timid, grave-tending life. It's adventurously expectant, **greeting God with a childlike "What's next, Papa?"** [emphasis mine]. God's Spirit touches our spirits and confirms who we really are. We know who he is, and we know who we are: Father and children. And we know we are going to get what's coming to us—an unbelievable inheritance! We go through exactly what Christ goes through. If we go through the hard times with him, then we're certainly going to go through the good times with him.

What a warm and loving relationship we enjoy as children of God. In a little bit, we are going to discuss how we far too often miss out on this intimate and assuring relationship with the Father and the Son.

The late David Wilkerson says this about "Abba Father":

The Holy Ghost has a way of simplifying our relationship with God the Father and Jesus. He is the One who teaches us to say, "Abba, Father." This phrase refers to an oriental custom of Bible days regarding the adoption of a child. Until the adopting papers were signed and sealed by the adopting father, the child saw this man only as a father. He had no right to call him Abba, meaning "my."

Yet, as soon as the papers were signed, registered, and sealed, the child's tutor presented him to the adopting father—and for the first time the child could say, "Abba, Father!" As the father embraced him, the young one cried, "My father! He's not just a father anymore. He's mine!" This is the work and ministry of the Holy Spirit. He tutors you of Christ. He presents you to the Father. And he keeps reminding you, "I have sealed the papers. You are no longer an orphan— you are legally a son of God! You now have a very loving, wealthy, powerful Father. Embrace him—call him 'my Father.' I have come to show you how much you're loved by him! He loved and wanted you!"

Our cry should be one of exceeding joy and
thanksgiving. The Spirit in us literally cries
out, "You are an heir, an inheritor of all that
Jesus won." And what an inheritance you have,
because your Father is the wealthiest in the whole
universe! Don't shy away from him; he's not mad
at you. Stop acting like an orphan who's poverty-
stricken, lacking joy and spiritual victory. **You are
not forsaken—so enjoy him!**" [emphasis mine].[35]

I John 3:1–3

The apostle and one of the original disciples of
Jesus, John, weighed in on this "Dad/Son" spiritual
relationship we enjoy as well.

> See what kind of love the Father has given to us
> that we should be *called children of God*; and so we
> are. The reason why the world does not know us
> is that it did not know him. Beloved, *we are God's
> children now*, and what we will be has not yet
> appeared; but we know that when he appears we
> shall be like him, because we shall see him as he
> is. And everyone who thus hopes in him purifies
> himself as he is pure. (ESV; italics mine)

Not only is God our faithful Father and "Papa" but
because He is, we are His beloved children—**now**,
not just later! I don't know what your earthly father
brought to the table, but I assure you, God the Father
is filled with love towards you—*now, this moment!*

---

[35] David Wilkerson, "David Wilkerson Devotions," *World
Challenge*, sermons.worldchallenge.org/en/view/devo-
tions?page=124.

Just as the hymn writer wrote, "How deep the Father's love for us, How vast beyond all measure; That He should give His only Son, To make a wretch His treasure [emphasis mine]."

That just about says it all. For the remainder of this chapter, let's look at the kind of Father you have always wanted and the one that you will find in God.

The Kind of Father You Have Always Wanted

Most of us would admit that we live in a world that is filled with fatherlessness and absentee fathers. Fathering is not an easy calling, and sad to say, many fathers in our world do not have the courage or the moral backbone to stand up and be counted—no matter what they are facing. It is interesting that the word "mother" is mentioned some 320 times from Genesis to Revelation in the King James Version of the Bible. But the word "father" is mentioned *1,103* times!

I agree with Dr. James Dobson, "Parenting isn't for cowards."[36] Neither is being a dad! It only takes a momentary biological urge of passion to be a father. Nothing to it, really! But it takes the love of God working in us and through us and the willingness to be a servant leader to be a dad that God can use and smile upon!

I don't know what kind of father you had growing up!

I know some of you had fathers who were and are still—the apple of your eye. Even if they have died and gone to heaven, when you think of your dad, it is mostly with warm and smiling memories. You are most blessed if that is your lot!

[36] James C. Dobson, *Parenting Isn't for Cowards* (Carol Stream, IL: Tyndale Momentum-Tyndale, 2007).

Others did not have the privilege of growing up with a dad, either because he passed from this life when they were very young or they were a casualty of divorce.

Maybe you had a father, but your relationship with him never got out of the "stranger or provider" stage, and your heart still has a hole in it that oozes sadness and regret. Others—and usually, this crowd is the largest—grew up with a father who was unkind, uncaring, absentee, or maybe downright abusive. Maybe not physically or even sexually (though that may be your experience), but he was abusive in a mental and emotional way, leaving you to battle with your feelings of whether you had value and worth—even as an adult.

I don't know where you are as you read this chapter. But God certainly does. He does not want you to live in the shadows of fear and rejection. Our past life with the absence of a loving, patient father does not have to rule us today. Just because your earthly father failed you and disappointed you time and time again does *not* mean that you are bound and enslaved to the spirit of defeat, depression, or mediocrity.

Eric Geiger writes:

Maybe you think you don't want another father. Been there, done that. And you would rather do without. Yet God insists on calling Himself you're Father. I love how Louie Giglio describes this tension:

"God is not the reflection of your earthly father. He is the perfection of your earthly Father." God is not the supersized version of your dad. He is not just the blown-up replica of your earthly father.

God is not your dad amplified in high definition and surround sound. Regardless of your earthly father's example, God is the perfect Father. And he is your Father. If you have trusted Him with your life and received Him as your Lord, He gave you the right to be His kid (John 1:12–13). Regardless of how you grew up, whether you had a great dad or a lousy deadbeat absentee father, whether you call someone on Father's Day or not, God is your perfect Father.

Alrighty, then. That rundown ought to put a pep in your step this day!

In a wonderful story that Jesus tells in Luke chapter 15, what we have come to call "The Story of The Prodigal Son" really is a story about a "Patient, Loving, and Accepting Father." I believe it is a mistake to put the emphasis on the "lost son." The emphasis and the hero of the story, in my humble opinion, **is not the returning Son, but the Loving Father who longed to love and receive back his son no matter what, no matter when!**

I want to point out in this story what your "Abba Father" is like—even on your darkest days of living or failing to live for Him:

1. Your Abba Father is a rich father.

"To illustrate the point further, Jesus told them this story: 'A man had two sons. The younger son told his father, 'I want my share of your estate now before you die.' *So his father agreed to divide his wealth between his sons*" (NLT; italics mine).

Did you know that your "heavenly Father" is rich where it counts? Did you know that your "heavenly

Father has made you an "heir" of God and a "joint heir" with his son, Jesus Christ?

What does that mean? Someone said it this way:

> If you were told that you were going to inherit a vast sum of money, what would you do? What would you think? How would you react? We Christians are sitting on a fortune and acting like paupers; we still behave with the same poor old nature; we do not live like we are children of the King; we think in terms of what we owe instead of what is already bought and paid for by the Lord Jesus Christ!

If you are a follower of Jesus, your heavenly Father has made you far richer than Bill Gates and Warren Buffet. Compared to you, they are dirt-poor. He is willing to divide his inheritance with you on the front end, no matter what you will do with it. *Think about that.*

2. Your Abba Father is a restrictive father.

> A few days later this younger son packed all his belongings and moved to a distant land, and there he wasted all his money in wild living. About the time his money ran out, a great famine swept over the land, and he began to starve. He persuaded a local farmer to hire him, and the man sent him into his fields to feed the pigs. The young man became so hungry that even the pods he was feeding the pigs looked good to him. *But no one gave him anything* (NLT; italics mine).

What do I mean by a "restrictive father"? I simply mean that if we as children of God want to do what we *want,* then God is not under any obligation to provide what we *need!* "But no one gave him anything" is part of what God will do when His children want their own way! Your heavenly Father has a way of bringing you down if you bring Him down. God has a way of bringing you to the *end of yourself* so that you can find your way back to Him. His favor rests on those who are "careful" with the treasure He has entrusted them with. "He who is faithful in little things," the Scriptures say, will be entrusted with much." You and I should be glad that our heavenly Father restricts us from finding joy and pleasure in anything else but Him. As our Abba Father, He is willing to call us the way we are, but He is not willing to let us stay there. And so, He faithfully paints us into a corner so that the only way we can turn is upward towards Him.

Look at verse 17 with me as we continue the story:

3. Your Abba Father is a reliable father.

> When he finally came to his senses, he said to himself, "At home even the hired servants have food enough to spare, and here I am dying of hunger! I will go home to my father and say, 'Father, I have sinned against both heaven and you, and I am no longer worthy of being called your son. Please take me on as a hired servant'" (NLT).

Did you know your heavenly Father is available 24/7? He is available all 365 days a year and every moment of every day? No matter where you are. Don't miss that. The Scriptures tell us that this prodigal, rebellious son said one day when he came to his senses, "I will go home to my father. . . ." It was a huge and courageous thing to do, but his decision was also filled with a lot of questions and fear of what may happen when he returned to the edge of the property!

Why did he make that decision? Because he knew his father would be waiting for him. He knew he had a reliable father he could count on back home!

Question: How much more do we have a "heavenly Papa" who is completely reliable and trustworthy? Hebrews tells us that God "will never leave us or forsake us" (Heb. 13:5). Jesus promised us that "He would be with us to the end of the age" (Matt. 28:20). The psalmist reminds us that God will "be with us and be our guide until death" (Ps. 45:10).

Verse 20 of Luke 15 reveals another amazing trait of this father:

4. Your Abba Father is a running father.

That is good news, don't you think?

"So he returned home to his father. And while he was still a long way off, his father saw him coming. Filled with love and compassion, he *ran* to his son, embraced him, and kissed him" (NLT; italics mine).

Bible scholars tell us that in the Middle East at that time, it was considered shameful and even humiliating for men over age forty to run in public. As the father ran, he would have had to lift his robe up, which brought further humiliation.

So here's a question that begs an answer: If it was so shameful for a man to run in that culture, then why did the father run towards his returning son? What would motivate him to bring shame upon himself? To understand this father's motivation, we need to understand an all-important first-century Jewish custom.

Kenneth Bailey, author of *The Cross & the Prodigal*, explains that if a Jewish son lost his inheritance among Gentiles and then returned home, the community would perform a ceremony, called the *kezazah*. They would actually break a large pot in front of him and yell, "You are now cut off from your people." The community would totally reject him. *So why did the father run?*

He probably ran in order to get his son *before* he entered the village. The father runs and shames himself in an effort to get to his son before the community gets to him so that his son does not experience the shame and humiliation of their taunting and rejection. The village that would have followed the running father would have witnessed what took place at the edge of the village between father and son. After this emotional reuniting of the prodigal son with his father, it was clear that there would be no kezazah ceremony; there would be no rejecting this son—*despite* what he had done. The son had repented and returned to the father. The father had taken the full shame that should have fallen upon his son and clearly showed the entire community that his son was welcome back home.

What an act of a loving daddy! Abba Papa, to be exact!

It was that act in this story—and one in *another* story—that depicts the great picture of love on the part of God the Father. On that one tree hill so very long ago, Jesus, God's Son, took on the shame and humiliation of all of us that we could be welcomed back into the family. Hebrews 12:3 says that Jesus despised [hated] the shame that he would have to endure, but for our lost eternal soul, even that was not too great of a cost. God is willing to "shame" Himself on a cross, and he is still willing to shame Himself in our lives *if* we would just turn our hearts toward home!

5. Your Abba Father is a restoring father.

"His son said to him, 'Father, I have sinned against both heaven and you, and I am no longer worthy of being called your son."

Isaiah 64:8–9 reminds us, "But now, O LORD, YOU ARE OUR FATHER; we are the clay, and you are our potter; we are all the work of your hand. Be not so terribly angry, O LORD, AND REMEMBER NOT INIQUITY FOREVER. Behold, please look, we are all your people" (ESV).

But the son (because of his sinful and fleshly living) no longer believed he was worthy to be a son in the father's family. That's what he said and that's what he believed. But notice the Father's *reaction* to his son's full-blown, heartfelt, fully rehearsed, confession:

But his father said to the servants, "Quick! Bring the finest robe in the house and put it on him. Get a ring for his finger and sandals for his feet. And kill the calf we have been fattening. We must celebrate with a feast, for this son of mine was dead and has now returned to life. He was lost, but now he is found." (NLT)

Now, here's how *we* often read it: But the father said you are going to pay me back every last dime you spent. And you're right: You need to work your way back into this family. You have been an embarrassment to this family, and it is going to take a long time for me to trust you again. Now get gone!

I want to remind you that God, your Father, is a "restoring" Father who gives you "beauty for ashes" and is willing to give you a place at the table again—gladly if you would recognize the family call bell again and respond. Aren't you *glad* today that this Father is a Father that takes us back each time we fail and fall? The psalmist said it right when he wrote, "If it had not been for the Lord, where would we be?" (Ps. 118:6).

6. Your Abba Father is a rejoicing father.

Verse 24 reads, "So the party began." That is a pretty profound statement when you think about it.

The Bible says that there is "great rejoicing" in heaven when a sinner changes his mind about God and comes to Him for salvation. Whenever a lost person or the child of God changes His mind (the Bible calls this "repentance") and heart about Christ and gets right with Him, the Father rejoices and smiles, and all of heaven goes into "party mode." That ought to answer a lot of questions on whether God is an ogre in the sky that is about to crush the human race at any given second!

In his book *The Kingdom Of God Is a Party,* Tony Campolo writes these powerful words about the straying son:

Now, if you're going to go home after blowing half of your father's wealth, you'd better rehearse your speech. All the way home he's practicing over and over again:

"Father, I have sinned against heaven and against thee. I am no longer worthy to be called your son." The Bible says his father sees him when he's yet a far distance far off, runs out, and throws his arms around him. The boy starts his little talk, "Father I have sinned against heaven and against thee—"

The father interrupts, "Harry, go get a robe and throw it on this kid. He's got rags."

"I am no longer worthy to be called thy son—"

"Jim, get a ring put it on his finger to celebrate this day!"

"Make me one of your—"

"Knock it off, son! Hey Bill, out behind the barn there's a fat calf. Kill that sucker. We're going to have a party! What time is it? It's party time!"

Zephaniah, the Old Testament prophet, encourages us with this verse, "The LORD your God is in your midst, a mighty one who will save; he will rejoice over you with gladness; he will quiet you by his love; he will rejoice over you with loud singing" (3:17, ESV). *You* may have not had an earthly father that loved having you around, but I can assure you that you have a Father in heaven who longs to spend time with you—every day, all day if need be! If He had a wallet, your picture would be in it— that I can guarantee you of. You are the apple of His eye.

The last principle from the story shows us the kind of father we have always wanted:

7. Your Abba Father is a reasonable father.

Verse 25 begins,

Now his older son was in the field, and as he came and drew near to the house, he heard music and dancing. And he called one of the servants and asked what these things meant. And he said to him, "Your brother has come, and your father has killed the fattened calf, because he has received him back safe and sound."

But he was angry and refused to go in. His father came out and entreated him, but he answered his father, "Look, these many years I have served you, and I never disobeyed your command, yet you never gave me a young goat that I might celebrate with my friends, but when this son of yours came, who has devoured your property with prostitutes, you killed the fattened calf for him!" And he said to him, "Son, you are always with me, and all that is mine is yours. It was fitting to celebrate and be glad, for this your brother was dead, and is alive; he was lost, and is found." (NLT)

Isaiah 1:18 says [God speaking], "Come now, let us reason together, says the LORD: though your sins are like scarlet, they shall be as white as snow; though they are red like crimson, they shall become like wool (ESV).

Romans 12:1 says, "I appeal to you therefore, brothers, by the mercies of God, to present your bodies as a living sacrifice, holy and acceptable to God, which is your spiritual worship" (ESV).

Your Father in heaven is a *reasonable* Father, which means that He is capable of balanced behavior and decisions. He has great judgment and is fair and true in all that He does towards us. That is the keystone of who He is. He is not this inflexible, impatient Father that the Devil seeks to paint for us. He is fair. He is just. He is for you and not against you (Rom. 8:31).

A young man was to be sentenced to prison. The judge had known him from childhood, for he was well acquainted with his father—a famous legal scholar and the author of an exhaustive study entitled *The Law of Trusts*.

"Do you remember your father?" asked the magistrate. "I remember him well, Your Honor," came the reply. Then, trying to probe the offender's conscience, the judge said, "As you are about to be sentenced and as you think of your wonderful dad, what do you remember most clearly about him?"

There was a pause. Then the judge received an answer he had not expected. "I remember when I went to him for advice. He looked up at me from the book he was writing and said, 'Run along, boy; I'm busy!" When I went to him for companionship, he turned me away, saying, 'Run along, son; this book must be finished!' Your honor, you remember him as a great lawyer. I remember him as a lost friend." The magistrate muttered to himself, "Alas! Finished the book, but lost the boy!"

Not this dad in Luke 15!

He was willing to deal with each child on their own level, and he would always seek to take his own child's feelings seriously! Those feelings and opinions may not be right, but they are real and felt deeply, and he recognizes them as such! So God our heavenly Father longs for us to come and pour out our hearts to Him. The Psalms are full of conversations that David had with God and they aren't all "pretty." But God is reasonable, and He will listen to us and reason with us so that we know that His way is always the best way!

Do you want your father telling you just what you *want* to hear or what you *need* to hear? The Proverbs tell us that "the wounds of a friend are faithful but the kisses of an enemy are deceitful." The Father says, "Son/ Daughter, you are always with me, and all that is mine is yours. It was fitting to celebrate and be glad, for this your brother was dead, and is alive; he was lost, and is found."

Isn't that a beautiful portrait of Abba Father? Please don't let another minute go by seeing the Father's love through your earthly father's love. It's maybe what you have been doing your whole life. It is what will keep you from moving forward in your faith. Believe God and His word and live—*really live!*

11

Preparing for Book #2

Well, we have completed the first book, but we have not completed the plan to have you understand and see the whole story. We still have some all-important ground to cover in the second book. Just think of this as halftime, and a second half is just around the corner. Remember, this study of the identity driven life is incomplete at this point. Did you hear what I said? While this first book certainly stands on its own as a life-changing Bible-filled truth document, you *have* to show up for the second half. You have to play a whole game. All sixty minutes. At the end of the game (post soon-coming book number two), you will be able to say that you now know where true identity comes from, why it is important to see yourself through God's eyes, and the importance of receiving forgiveness from God and giving it to others. That is a mouthful, but it is what we are going to really bring home in the second book.

Let me share some "bullet point" reminders from this first installment so we can not only end on the same page but also be ready to pick up where we left off when the second book is available.

Chapter Highlights in Review

• Chapter 1: The identity driven life is a clear call to all those who identify with Christ to find their identity in Christ. I like to say it this way: Knowing who you are (identity) is just as important as knowing why you are (purpose). Both are important to living a successful Christian life, but one has to come before the other.

• Chapter 2: God wants you and me to know that "we" as His beloved children are the apple of His eye, and what He says and feels about us matters most.

• Chapter 3: So, what is God's order in the New Testament as it relates to our new identity in Christ?

To begin with, we must understand (and Jesus made it clear) that what happens *in* us is of far more value than what happens *to* us or even comes *from* us. Put another way, what God has done *in* us and what He chooses to do *through* us is to be valued most *by* us. *Why?* Simply because if the source of our strength and success is rooted in Christ, He will get all the glory and credit He rightfully deserves, and that is good news for us. That is what the identity driven life embodies; it is also why our spiritual foundation is what really counts most in this life.

• Chapter 4: Your greatest challenge as you read this book is to stay the course. Deal with the pain that God brings to the surface. Refuse to believe the lies of the enemy any longer.

• Chapter 5: To most people, and even to most Christians, Christianity is what I call "an add-on" religion rather than a way of life. For far too many years, it has become a faith that is characterized by things that you *do* rather than a vibrant, living faith that focuses on the character of what you *become* because of the faith that you hold.

• Chapter 6: If we are ever going to be all that God desires; if we are ever going to be at peace with ourselves and God; if we are ever going to get past the deep ruts and healing from the scarring incisions of our past, we are going to have to believe what God says about us. Why shouldn't we? For a lifetime, we have believed the lies the Devil has been dealing out. Many of us have mistakenly built our lives on shifting, undependable sand rooted in a core belief that says our worth and value is in "us." That we must become the best version of ourselves. That in "us" and our strength, we have the power to become all that God intended. Those lies have made us look good on the outside (at least some of us) but have kept us usefully reckless and broken in our spiritual influence. God made us to know Him intimately, and the only way we can do that is to believe Him without reservation.

• Chapter 7: In the spiritual realm, it is who you *really* are, not who *others* think you are or even who *you* think you are. We've got to be convinced that what God thinks is really the chief thing that matters when all is said and done! He is the final voice on the matter. If you question that, do you have anyone else that would be qualified to make this determination? If God is the most powerful person in the universe and He knows all things, don't you think what He says should be strongly considered and adopted quickly?

• Chapter 8: The key to spiritual freedom is found in casting out the lies of Satan and replacing them with the truth of God found in His Word, the Bible. Your feelings and the lies that you have cuddled up to over the years offer no spiritual help when it comes to spiritual freedom. Don't take that statement lightly.

• Chapter 9: The cross is the exclamation point on what the Scriptures say about God's amazing love! You want to know if or how much God loves you in Christ? Just be brave enough to glance at the cross.

• Chapter 10: Understanding our true identity in Christ begins with an honest assessment of who God exactly is. Now, God is a lot of things, to be sure, and His person is really past finding out fully, but in talking about all the grand and great truths about the greatness and the loftiness of God, a heartwarming and emotionally charged biblical portrait of God emerges. This portrait, if we are not careful, will be overlooked, unappreciated, and in the end, ignored. If it is, we will run the race that God has set before us empty, discouraged, and emotionally and spiritually detached from the kind of life that God intended when He made us.

We welcome this portrait's entrance into our lives, but its entrance is a rough and difficult one. It is mainly because so many of us are so scarred from our early years and from the decisions that we have made apart from the wisdom of God in our adult life. This is pretty heavy language, but I'm just keeping it real. We have the love of God neatly stored in our cranium, but it is often a distant stranger at the core of our being. There is definitely an "eighteen-inch" difference in our understanding (the distance between the head and the heart). This portrait that needs to be hung on every heart is the truth of God as our heavenly Dad! Without it, we can never become the child of God that God desires and longs for us to be. And that is tragic!

I have spent most of my adult life attempting to point others to the Greatest Healer of all, the Lord Jesus Christ. I can't heal anyone. Yet, I have come to know Someone who can, and really, when it gets right down to it, **He loves to do so.** It was one of the chief reasons He came to this earth (Luke 4:19–21; Gal. 5:1).

I want to encourage you to read this book again before the second one comes out. And please share it with someone else. I know that these truths are not easy to grasp in this culture, and that includes our church culture. Although the second book will really complement and bring into focus the "rest of the story," digesting what you have read in this first book will greatly help you get or stay spiritually free for the rest of your days.

In his book *Growing In Grace*, Bob George tells the story of "J. E.":

When you first met "J. E.," you could tell he was a very angry man. In fact, at age fifty-four, he'd been an angry person for many years. In a Bible study that night, many questions had been raised in his mind. Talking with the leader afterward, J. E. said, "I asked Jesus to be my Savior when I was nine years old. But nobody ever taught me about whom I am in Christ, that I'm accepted by God, or that Christ lives in me."

"What were you taught?" the Bible study leader asked. "Where I grew up, we heard all the time about how perfect Christ was and about how we should learn to live like Him—if we didn't, God would judge us." J. E. went on, "It didn't take me long, I'd say in my teen years, to figure out that I was never going to cut it. So I gave up trying. I guess I've been living in guilt and running from God ever since. Off and on through the years, I tried to go back to church, but I just got more guilt piled on top of me. I've sat under so many teachers who made me fearful that I was afraid to turn in any direction, because God was going to get me. This is the first Bible study I've ever attended that gave me any hope," J. E. concluded.

At that point, J. E. was fifty-four years old. That means, even though he had been born again through trusting Jesus Christ at a young age, he had spent at least thirty-five years running away from God. Tragically, his experience isn't that unusual. Thousands of people who sincerely responded to the gospel message they were taught spend years thrashing around trying to make it work, but without success. In fact, I believe the reason so many Christians struggle in living the Christian life is their lack of understanding their *Identity in Christ* [italics mine].[37]

Do you get George's last sentence? Read it again. That is the reason you have read this book and the reason why I wrote it.

See you again—the second half!

[37] Bob George, *Growing in Grace* (Eugene, OR: Harvest House, 1991), n.p.

Scripture Index & Scriptural Inferences

Exodus 34:6

1 Chronicles 16:34

Psalms 31:21; 45:10; 115:3; 118:6

Proverbs 23:7; 29:18

Isaiah 1:18; 53:2-3; 63:9; 64:6; 64:8-9

Jeremiah 9:23-24; 31:3; 33:3

Habakkuk 1:13

Zephaniah 3:17

Matthew 5:13-16; 6:33; 22:16; 28:19-20

Luke 4:19-21; 6:47-48; 9:23-25; 10:1-20; 15:15-32; 16:15

John 1:12; 1:14; 1:17; 3:16-18; 3:30; 8:31-36; 8:44; 10:10; 14:6; 15:1,5; 15:13; 15:15; 16:13; 17:17; 18:37

Acts 1:8; 20:35

Romans 1:1-7; 1:25; 5:1; 5:5; 5:8; 6:1-2; 6:6; 6:14-23; 6:18-22; 6:23; 8:1; 8:15-17; 8:28-32; 8:31; 8:37; 8:35-39; 10:4; 11:29; 12:1; 12:2

I Corinthians 1:1-3 (AMP); 1:26;1:27; 2:16; 3:11; 6:17; 6:19-20; 10:4; 12:27; 15:10; 15:32

II Corinthians 2:16; 5:9; 5:17; 5:18; 5:20; 5:21; 12:7-10

Galatians 2:20; 2:19-21; 5:1; 5:16-21; 5:22

Ephesians 1:1; 1:3; 1:5; 1:11(Msg) 1:13; 1:18; 2:3; 2:6; 2:9; 2:10; 2:18; 2:19-21; 3:18-19; 4:1; 4:11-14; 4:20-21; 6:10-18; 6:14

Philippians 1:6; 2:9-10; 3:20; 4:13

Colossians 1:13; 1:12-13; 1:14; 1:15-21; 1:28; 2:6-10 (AMP); 2:10; 2:13-15; 3:3; 3:4;3:12

Second Thessalonians 1:11; 2:10-13

I Timothy 2:4; 6:8-11, 16-18

2 Timothy 1:7; 1:9; 2:15; 4:4

Titus 3:5

Hebrews 2:13-15; 3:1; 5:13-14; 12:1; 12:3-12; 13:5

James 1:5; 1:18; 2:1-10; 4:8; 5:20

1 Peter 1:1-2; 1:3-16; 2:11; 2:9-12; 5:5

2 Peter 1:3-4; 1:5-11

1 John 1:6-8; 2:19; 3:1-3; 3:16; 4:4; 4:7-10; 4:17; 5:18

Jude 1:20-21

Revelation 1:4-6; 3:14-21; 3:20